PRACTICAL KNOWLEDGE ENGINEERING

creating

successful

commercial

expert

systems

Practical Knowledge Engineering

RICHARD V. KELLY JR.

Digital Press

Printed in the United States of America

9 8 7 6 5 4 3 2 1

Order number EY-H874E-DP

Design: Sandra Calef
Production: Editorial Services of New England, Inc.
Composition: Editorial Services of New England, Inc., using Ventura Publisher
Printer: Hamilton Printing Company

On the cover: Piet Mondrian. *Broadway Boogie Woogie.* 1942-43. Oil on canvas, 50" x 50". Collection, The Museum of Modern Art, New York. Photograph © 1991 by The Museum of Modern Art, New York.

Library of Congress Cataloging-in-Publication Data

Kelly, Richard V.
    Practical knowledge engineering : creating successful commercial expert systems / by Richard V. Kelly, Jr.
        p.   cm.
    Includes bibliographical references and index.
    ISBN 1-55558-070-X (pbk.)
    1. Expert systems (Computer science) 2. Software engineering.
I. Title.
QA76.76.E95K435   1991
006.3'3—dc20   91-8208
                                                   CIP

Contents

Preface

This is a book about knowledge engineering, the task of building successful commercial expert systems. It is intended as a record of what actually works (and doesn't work) in the construction of commercial expert systems. It is based on the author's nine years of experience in building expert systems in large and small organizations, in all major areas of application, for American, Japanese, and European corporations.

In this book, "expert system" refers to any computer program which emulates human problem-solving abilities, especially by heuristic methods, and which offers recommendations for action or commits actions based upon its understanding of the problem to be solved.

This book is intended for anyone involved in the development of commercial expert systems, especially anyone laboring under the title of "knowledge engineer"—broadly defined as someone with responsibility for the development, management, implementation, and maintenance of expert systems. The author's hope is that the book will be used as a map of *terra incognita* by those just beginning to develop expert systems, and by practicing knowledge engineers searching for solutions to particular problems.

The book is arranged according to the stages of development typical to an expert system project: from initial selection of the problem to be solved, through design and construction, to final presentation of the system.

The introductory chapter addresses the question, "What is knowledge engineering?" and focuses on the daily concerns and skill requirements of knowledge engineers, who work in a field that encompasses several discrete disciplines.

The second chapter, "Frequently Asked Questions," answers questions most often asked by knowledge engineers in training, managers, expert system users, and project funders.

Chapter 3, "Prospecting," is an aid to selecting problems suitable for solution by an expert system. It lists and explains the practical questions that should be asked when new expert system development is being considered.

Chapter 4, "Beginning a Project," suggests methods for initiating the development of expert systems and points out the pitfalls to be avoided.

The fifth chapter, "Paradigms and Purposes," details how expert systems are categorized according to the type of problem they solve, the use they are put to, and the industry in which they are used.

Chapter 6, "Knowledge Acquisition," focuses on the techniques used by knowledge engineers to solicit the greatest degree of cooperation and information from domain experts.

Chapter 7, "Knowledge Representation," explains the major knowledge representation schemes via specific expert system application examples.

Chapter 8, "Costing, Metrics, and Specification," illustrates how knowledge engineers can chart the progress of their system and manage its growth.

Chapter 9, "Knowledge Engineering Techniques," explains the practical methods used by knowledge engineers in the programming of expert systems.

Chapter 10, "Common Problems," details the problems most likely to result in the failure or abandonment of an expert system development project. It also contains brief case studies of actual failures.

And the last chapter, "Demonstrating an Expert System," gives pointers on presenting an expert system lucidly and succinctly to users and funders.

Appendix A, "A Case Study," is a knowledge engineer's analysis of one expert system development project from start to finish. It begins with the search for an appropriate application and ends with the completed expert system's implementation.

Appendix B, "Tool Selection," is not a listing of currently popular tool offerings, but a method by which to evaluate the suitability of any tool to be used in building an expert system.

Appendix C, "Knowledge Engineer Selection," offers some suggestions on what to look for when interviewing knowledge engineers for entry into an in-house AI group.

The contention made throughout this book is that, in a commercial setting, the knowledge engineer's job encompasses every facet of expert system development, not just coding and the interviewing of experts. If an expert system is to succeed, it is as much a knowledge engineer's job to ensure that the system is implemented as it is to map out knowledge representation schemes or link expert systems to conventional programs. And success is defined here as the creation of expert systems that are implemented to solve legitimate business problems. Expert systems which "work" but are not used are only academic exercises. An expert system that does not bring some practical return on investment by being *used* is valueless in a commercial environment.

The knowledge engineer is not the only person responsible for the success of an expert system development project. Concerned managers, patient users willing to offer feedback, domain experts who are magnanimous with their valuable time, talented MIS and field engineers, other knowledge engineers involved in the project (not all expert system projects are single knowledge engineer jobs), and supportive secretaries and administrative assistants all have a hand in every successful project. But knowledge engineers—although they necessarily must rely on all these groups and individuals—cannot afford to concentrate solely on programming and leave the management, logistics, implementation issues, and maintenance in the hands of other people.

Most commercial expert systems falter or fail for reasons of politics, personality, and human factors, not because of technical problems. A knowledge engineer working on commercial systems is required to attend to the human factors as well as to technical ones.

It is hoped that this book will be of benefit to those expert system builders trying to balance and respond to all the tasks involved in knowledge engineering.

Richard V. Kelly, Jr.
March, 1991

Acknowledgments

For their help in the creation of this book, I humbly express my gratitude to Joel Magid, George Horesta, Dave Cavallo, Paul Anagnostopoulos, David Steiers, Gary Hasman, Steve Gutz, Jay Shaughnessey, Andy Bennett, Dan Bogaty, Ram Josyula, Leslie Chesler, Lisa Spielman, Berge Sarkissian, Clint Bissell, Tanya Bruce, Martin Rooney, Bob Evans, Tom Cooper, Nancy Wogrin, Cathy Sheppard, Charise Sary, Ron Gaudet, Joe Parrillo, Jeff Neilan, Hanh Pham, Stan Wozniak, Terry Eccles, Carol-lee Erikson, Ping Shyr, Steve O'Hara, John Lawson, Forrest Wasserman, Nathan Law, Basil Horangic, Tom McBride, Lee Stommes, Takeshi Yabe, Toshio Tanaka, Carsten Collatz, Tam Pham, Roberto Piuzzo, Rosemary Baer, Mike Sarni, Bruno de Lorenzis, Bruce Kirkpatrick, Byoung-Mo Koo, Shigeru Tani, Sharri Magid, Athena Vitale, and Bandicoot Kelly.

R.V. K.

Introduction 1

What Is Knowledge Engineering?

Knowledge engineering is the task of building expert systems. And a knowledge engineer is someone who does everything necessary to guarantee the success of an expert system development project, including

- initiation

- management

- coding

- and maintenance of the system

Knowledge engineering involves the entire process of expert system development, including

- acquisition (getting the knowledge)

- representation (structuring the knowledge)

- prototyping (testing the knowledge)

- delivery (transferring the knowledge)

The knowledge engineer (KE) assumes a number of roles during a system's creation. On any given day, for example, a KE may be required to carry out one of the following tasks:

- prospect for suitable applications
- explain knowledge representation to project funders
- code the integration linkages between an inference engine, a knowledgebase, and a database
- demonstrate a well-developed prototype to users
- interview domain experts
- plan the expansion of systems already in operation

As a result, KEs have become technological generalists. They straddle the line between the science of cognitive psychology and the art of programming. Their job demands scholarship, logical and linguistic abilities, and an intuitive understanding of their fellow human beings.

What distinguishes knowledge engineering from other software engineering pursuits is the remarkable breadth of knowledge and skills required of its practitioners. A commercial knowledge engineer ordinarily takes on the responsibilities of

- traditional programmer
- project manager
- user representative
- systems analyst
- any new roles which result from the expert system development process

Despite all the skills it requires, knowledge engineering is not an arcane academic discipline. It is a practical set of techniques and an empirically derived body of knowledge. It is a methodology, a system for solving sophisticated business problems.

Tasks

Knowledge engineers are sometimes perceived as glorified programmers/analysts who interview experts in a particular domain, decompose gleaned information into a format understandable by an expert system, and encode a knowledgebase of rules. But this simple view of knowledge engineering is often entirely foreign to the daily experience of practicing KEs. This ordinary perception fails to account for the KE who, without ever interviewing an expert, builds an inductive inference engine that draws conclusions from cases stored in a database. It fails to account for the KE in a small, burgeoning artificial intelligence (AI) group who spends as much time demonstrating and marketing expert systems in-house as building them. And it fails to consider the KEs who find their expert systems so successful and well received that their time is consumed managing one existing system and its inevitable offshoots.

With the understanding, then, that there is no "typical" knowledge engineer, a KE is likely to be involved in the following areas:

- consultation (advising project funders, managers, users, and experts on the uses and positioning of expert systems within their organization)

- problem selection and project initiation (done in cooperation with managers, users, and experts)

- knowledge elicitation and acquisition (at first done largely with experts, but later with users as well)

- system design and architecture (usually done by the KE alone, but also with database administrators and management information system (MIS) managers when the expert system is highly integrated)

- tool selection (which depends on the budget, representation schemes, the application's paradigm and purpose, and in-house political factors)

- coding (a lonely business)

- coordination of the contributions made by various project participants

- management, maintenance, and expansion of the expert system

- demonstration of the system to concerned parties (usually more than once)

Comparisons

Expert System Development versus DP, MIS, and SP

The differences between commercial expert systems and conventional programs—data processing (DP), management information (MIS), and scientific programming (SP)—are generally differences of degree.

Conventional business programs, which usually do not explain their reasoning to users, deal more often with numbers and merged/sorted data that are collected to perform calculations (for example, space shuttle trajectories) or to produce lists (for example, payroll programs that write employee checks in batch mode).

Conventional applications usually deal with problems to which there is only one correct answer, and that answer is found by applying algorithms and formulas.

Ideally, conventional programs are revised as seldom as possible, and the programs' designers generally spec out as much of the problem as possible before committing their ideas to code.

Expert systems, on the other hand, deal more often with ideas and symbols that are used to make decisions, generally in realtime, on the screen rather than in batch mode (often with a log kept of the system's reasoning and its recommendations). There may be more than one "correct" answer to the problem the application solves, and decisions are made by inference, rather than application of formulas. Expert systems are expected to be constantly revised during development (prototyping), and specifications and metrics are generally created as a system is being built (iterative specification and successive approximation), rather than entirely at the project's inception. An expert system also usually offers the user some explanation of its reasoning or recommendations.

Expert Systems versus OR/LP Programming

From a KE's standpoint, operations research/linear programming (OR/LP) represents an iterative testing approach to problem solution: many possible solutions to a problem are rapidly tested and the non-failing answers are the right ones. An operations researcher asks the question "What would happen if we did this?" exhaustively until most of the possible solutions to a problem have been sifted through algorithmically.

OR methods occasionally can be disappointing, though. Combinatorial explosion may become a problem (too many possibilities to wade through in a short time). Human (domain expert) idiosyncracies may play a more important role in problem solution than statistics (when experts choose a particular solution for personal experiential, non-quantifiable reasons, rather than for algorithmic validity). And OR/LP can become too CPU-intensive to be cost effective (crunching through scores of possible solutions may require far more expensive computer power than quicker heuristic methods). But OR and expert system occasionally tackle the same types of problems, such as options trading/timing, CIM (computer integrated manufacture) process control, and telecommunications network configuration.

In general, an expert system will be the preferred method of solution in the following situations:

- When a problem is underspecified. If there are too few criteria upon which to make a decision and, therefore, too many possible solutions, an OR approach may be limited. In such a case, a backward chaining expert system that hypothesizes a solution based on whatever data it has collected might be preferable to the simulation method, which may require greater specificity to generate a solution.

- When decisions are to be based on hazy symbolic input rather than on precise numerical data (for example, "The potato chip is 'too crispy.' How do we adjust the oil-vat mass/temperature ratio to correct for the low water content of these potatoes?" rather than "Of all the possible oil-vat mass/temperature/water-content ratios, which one yields the chip of appropriate statistical crispiness?")

- When the question to be asked is not "Here are the raw data. How do we grind through them to come up with a solution?" but "How do we discover the associations among the raw data?" (for example, through an inductive expert system).

A Non-Technical Illustration

Consider the simple problem of locating the seeds in an orange. The OR/LP approach is to slice the fruit several hundred times horizontally and vertically, noting at which depth and breadth seeds are encountered. The DP/MIS approach is to remove the seeds, sort them by weight and girth, record the results in a database, and produce a report listing their features. The expert system approach is to first understand some of the relevant facts of orange biology:

- An orange is naturally divided into wedges of roughly uniform size.

- A single seed generally forms at the middle inner edge of each wedge.

- The number of wedges can be assumed from the circumference and variety of the orange.

It then infers from these guidelines the location and number of seeds.

Characteristics of a Successful KE

Successful commercial KEs share certain traits. The ten most noticeable of these characteristics, which, of course, are not limited to KEs, are listed below:

1. Successful KEs work well with people, even irritable, difficult people. They are good at drawing people out and are natural interviewers. They are extremely patient but just as persistent. They know how to read people and are able to sense confusion and intransigence as well as comprehension and acceptance. And they are often natural teachers, comfortable explaining what they are doing at whatever level of detail is appropriate to the listener.

2. Successful KEs are advocates for the users of their expert systems. They never foist a system on the unwilling, bulldoze the hesitant, or browbeat the reluctant. They cultivate a sense of trust between themselves and users, experts, managers, and other KEs.

3. Successful KEs know that an expert system is of no value if it is not being used, no matter how clever the code is. They see practicality (from the user's standpoint) as more important than the sophistication or elegance of the code. And they see user satisfaction as the only way of guaranteeing that the expert system—the fruit of their hard work—will be put to use.

4. Successful KEs never recommend the development of an expert system when a simpler, less expensive solution exists. They see expert systems as only one method of problem solution, and they know that other methods (DP/MIS, SP, OR/LP) are more appropriate in certain circumstances. They do not imply that expert systems are a panacea.

5. Successful KEs have no tolerance for hyperbole, prevarication, pretense, backslapping, or gladhanding. They develop reputations for technical knowledge, tenacity, and sincerity.

6. Successful KEs recognize that all organizations have a unique group culture, from small work teams to entire corporations, and they accept and learn to work within those different cultures. They learn the reward/punishment systems in place in a group and in individuals (for example, travel may be a reward or a punishment to different individuals under different circumstances) and they act accordingly.

7. Successful KEs are more impressed by genuine practical problem-solving skills than by academic credentials. They respect the abilities of the shop foreman who gets the downed cold-steel-rolling mill working again, the foreign exchange trader who generates profit by keeping a finger on the pulse of a global market, and the network diagnostician who fixes telecommunication collapses under pressure.

8. Successful KEs are comfortable with their own ignorance, knowing that they will inevitably appear unsophisticated in a new domain until they have at least picked up the jargon. But they learn quickly and easily. They enjoy learning, knowing that they themselves must become adept at every task they build a system in. And they strive for breadth of experience, sometimes concentrating on certain domains or paradigms, but never to the exclusion of the chance to learn a new language, tool, domain, or technique.

9. Successful KEs are able to delay their own gratification—their own desire for immediate palpable accomplishment—knowing that a system may require years of effort before it reaches its full potential. But they show results (prototype code) as soon as possible. And they enjoy the sense of process—of working toward a distant goal—as much as the sense of completion when the goal is reached.

10. Successful KEs consider themselves "renaissance people" rather than only "technical people." They do well at the tasks generalists are comfortable with (such as tying together a hundred threads of information from a dozen different groups contributing to a project, or getting a system out the door by dancing political waltzes around barriers put up by an organization). But they are consummate programmers as well.

Erudition is the opiate of the pedants.
Uzbeki knowledge engineering epigram

Frequently Asked Questions   *2*
The Knowledge Engineer as Consultant

Questions are inevitable whenever expert systems are introduced into an organization. Some of these questions are asked often enough by users, funders, managers, and experts to be predictable. Such recurring questions demonstrate the common concerns of all who have a stake in the development of an expert system. And these questions often demand an answer from a knowledge engineer before development of a system can even begin.

This chapter answers some of the questions, varying in complexity from the elementary to the arcane, that are most frequently asked of knowledge engineers introducing expert systems into an organization.

"Could you briefly describe what expert systems do, what they look like, and how they're built?"

A *commercial expert system* is a computer program which analyzes information and makes decisions. Its purpose, when all is said and done, is to solve business problems inferentially and to make or save money.

Commercial expert systems are usually categorized in one of three ways: by *domain*, by *paradigm*, or by *purpose*. The "domain" is the area of application in which the system is working, such as manufacturing, telecommunications, or financial services. "Paradigm" refers to the type of problem being addressed by the system, for example,

8

scheduling, diagnosis, anomaly detection, outlier analysis, or configuration. "Purpose" includes advice giving (*advisory* and *consultancy* systems), the replacement of human decision makers (*proxy* systems), or the creation of new expertise in a given field (often by *induction*).

It is possible, then, to describe a particular application according to any one, two, or all three categories. For example, a system which makes recommendations on hospital procedures that exceed fixed payments (medical costs greater than what Medicare will pay) may be described as a "Hospital Administration Cost-Containment (domain) Diagnosis and Outlier Analysis (paradigms) Advisory (purpose) expert system."

Structure

Expert systems have two major components: a *knowledgebase* and an *inference engine*. (Most systems also contain some form of *user interface*, but not all. Process control expert systems, for example, can accept data from machinery sensors, make decisions based on the data, and invoke the necessary machinery adjustments directly and automatically.) The knowledgebase usually contains the distillation of a human expert's experience in a particular field. The inference engine picks through the knowledgebase to decide on the appropriate actions to take in a given circumstance.

The components of an expert system are ordinarily coded separately. When this is done, the same inference engine can be used on other similar problems simply by substituting appropriate knowledgebases. Such an engine may eventually be made so generic in scope that it becomes a *domain-independent* or *paradigm-specific development tool*, a tool that can be used to build expert systems in any field of knowledge (domain independent) or in one particular paradigm (paradigm specific).

Input and Output

The information that an expert system needs to make its decisions may be drawn directly from machinery *sensors* (as in the process control applications that monitor the performance of manufacturing equipment) or from *livefeeds/direct feeds* (as in the realtime market monitors used by bond traders). Or a user may input the information via keyboard in response to questions asked by the expert system. Sometimes several methods are employed together.

An expert system's output may include warnings, recommendations, instructions to the user, graphical displays, or direct action on a problem.

Reasons for Building Expert Systems

Expert systems generally are built to solve certain common decision-making problems. They are built when there are too many possible choices in a given situation and it would take too long to consider all of the alternatives (for example, 100,000,000 ways in which to configure a large computer network). This type of problem is called *combinatorial explosion*.

Expert systems often are built to distribute the expertise of people whose skills are rare (for example, a telecommunications network diagnostician who is on call 24 hours a day and would rather have an expert system on call nights and weekends). And expert systems also are built so that everyone doing a particular job (for instance, diagnosing customer problems over the phone at a *help desk* or a hotline) has access to the same level of expertise as the best problem solvers in the company (whose knowledge is incorporated into the knowledgebase).

Inference

Regardless of the reason for their being built, most expert systems employ an *inference method* to make decisions. The most common inference method is *deduction*, the process of reaching conclusions from propositions.

Deductive systems usually begin with knowledge of a domain and apply what they know about that domain in general to individual problems. A meteorological system to predict severe convective storms, for example, may "know" that hail and tornadoes are extremely rare at night. It may then chart the course of a cyclone through a geographic area and predict that that particular storm will not enter populated areas because night will fall before the storm can travel to them. Such a deductive system uses its knowledge of convective storms (in the form of general rules of storm behavior) to predict the behavior of one particular tornado. It deduces the particular storm's behavior.

Within the deductive inference method, two reasoning strategies are commonly used: *backward chaining* and *forward chaining*. Backward chaining systems usually ask questions of the user, make an assumption (a *hypothesis*) about what the user-provided data mean, and then try to prove that assumption by asking more focused questions. Forward chaining systems, on the other hand, doggedly and steadily collect data along the way toward reaching an eventual final hypothesis.

Project Flow

The process of building an expert system begins with *prospecting*, the act of identifying problems amenable to solution by an expert system. Once a system has been selected, the iterative task of *prototyping* begins. Eventually the system is implemented after final *integration linkages* to conventional systems or to other expert systems have been made. Of all the tasks involved in constructing an expert system, prototyping requires the greatest time and effort.

The prototyping of a deductive expert system is a continuous process of interviewing *domain experts* with experience in a particular field, a task known as *knowledge acquisition*. Part of this process involves coaxing out of the expert *deep knowledge* and *surface knowledge*, sometimes thought of as "theoretical" and "experiential" knowledge, respectively.

After some initial knowledge acquisition, *coding* of the system begins. Coding often produces a first working prototype within several weeks of the first interview. The coded prototype is then shown to the experts (and, later, to users), and comments are solicited. The system then begins to be transmuted according to the suggestions of the experts and the users.

At the end of this long iterative cycle, development is temporarily halted and the system is made operational, that is, it is *frozen* and put into production. The system is then developed further to enhance its functionality, employed as is, or both.

Project Participants

The cast of characters involved in the development of an expert system may include a project funder, a domain expert, users of the finished system, knowledge engineers to be trained or worked with as colleagues, and a project manager. Most often, the true project manager's role is assumed by the KE, who understands both the technical details and the personnel issues involved in developing the system.

"What are the most common types of expert systems?"

The following list is a breakdown of the expert system development projects one knowledge engineer (the author) had a hand in over the course of three typical years (in roles which included simple managerial consultation, the teaching of novice KEs, coding of integration linkages, and extensive knowledge acquisition, representation, and coding of inference engines and knowledgebases).

Projects: 45

Companies: 45

Locations of companies: U.S., 24; Non-U.S., 21 (Australia, 1; Canada, 3; France, 2; Germany, 2; Holland, 1; Hong Kong, 1; Italy, 2; Japan, 4; Korea, 2; Spain, 1; Switzerland, 1; UK, 1)

Domains

Manufacturing: 16

   (Consumer and industrial products, 9; Steel, 4; Pharmaceuticals, 3)

Telecommunications: 8

Financial services: 8

Software engineering: 4

Energy transmission: 2

Computer network security/maintenance: 2

Food processing: 2

Other (resource exploration, meteorology, construction): 3

Paradigms

Diagnosis/classification: 18

Interpretation/analysis: 9

Configuration/selection: 6

Anomaly detection/monitoring/prediction: 4

Design: 4

Scheduling/planning: 4

Hybrid projects: 4 (simulation with configuration, database analysis with design, spatial reasoning with analysis, image recognition/analysis)

OPS5: 25

Nexpert: 16

FORTRAN: 15

GKS (Graphical Kernal System): 8

C: 6

LISP: 5

MERCURY: 3

DCL (Digital Command Language): 3

FMS (Forms Management System): 2

EPITOOL: 1

ART-IM: 1

UDS (User-Oriented Diagnostic System): 1

BASIC: 1

COBOL: 1

Pascal: 1

RDB (Relational Database): 1

RIO: 1

SCAN: 1

TRELLIS/OWL: 1

PAM (Parallel Associative Memory): 1

Percentage of projects using more than one language in the expert system: 91 (most common combinations: (OPS5/FORTRAN/ GKS, Nexpert/C)

Percentage of expert systems which were integrated into existing or new conventional applications: 97

These figures are not part of a scientific survey. They are simply data collected by one KE working in one large expert system development group. Undoubtedly, statistical and practical biases are built into these data. So the conclusions reached from this information are certainly disputable. But since no attempt was made at any stage of the prospecting process to restrict or encourage the construction of expert systems in any particular domain or paradigm, these systems are likely to be representative of the types of commercial expert systems being built at this time.

What these figures do imply is that *it is almost impossible to build a truly standalone expert system or an expert system that makes use of only one programming language.*

"How is a KE's time usually divided up?"

The following survey was made of practicing KEs. It does not purport to be a statistically pure or unbiased analysis, but it is probably representative of the time put into certain tasks by the majority of knowledge engineers.

A KE's Schedule

	Percentage of Time	
Task	Average	Range
Prospecting (selecting appropriate applications)	4	0–10
Prototyping		
Specification/review/management (formal project management)	7	3–15
Knowledge acquisition (interviewing domain experts)	14	7–25
Knowledge representation/modeling (determining inference strategies and representation schemes)	11	8–17
Programming (writing, testing, revising code)	45	25–80
Implementation and technology transfer (user education, coordination with other KEs and programmers, consultation, managerial guidance, handholding)	12	3–20
Integration/hybridization (linkage to other expert or conventional systems)	20	0–50

These figures imply that the majority of a KE's time is spent programming and, when necessary, integrating expert systems with conventional programs or other expert systems. They also point to the comparatively large amount of time spent in helping users feel comfortable with an expert system and the comparatively limited amount of time spent in *formal* project management.

"What is knowledge representation?"

The task of deciding how to structure and manipulate knowledge in an expert system is called *knowledge representation*. The simplest division of knowledge in an expert system is between *declarative* and *procedural* knowledge. Knowledge stored as facts and statements is declarative. Knowledge about what to do with those facts and statements is procedural. For example,

"The offered downpayment is insufficient"

is declarative.

"IF the offered downpayment is insufficient for this mortgage,
THEN suggest a higher-interest-rate mortgage package"

is procedural.

In an expert system's knowledgebase, declarative knowledge often takes the form of *object-attribute-value (O-A-V) triplets*, for example, "sandstone method-of-formation sedimentary." The object is the name of the item itself ("sandstone"). The attribute is the property of that item ("method-of-formation"). And the value ("sedimentary") is the degree, rate, or worth of the attribute. O-A-V triplets can often be read as "The *attribute* of the *object* is *value*" (in this case, "the method-of-formation of sandstone is sedimentary")

Both declarative and procedural knowledge can be categorized by their *granularity*. Granularity is the degree of detail in a fact or rule.

If the apples are ripe
Then I pick them

is a *large-grained* rule.

If the date is after September 19
and the apple variety is Cox's Orange Pippin
and there was no hard frost during fruit set
and plum curculio infestation was minimal

and the fruit is beyond first breaking blush stage
Then I pick them

is a *fine-grained* rule.

When to apply the knowledge in this knowledgebase of apple-harvesting rules is a *meta-knowledge* problem. For example, the rule above may be contained in a knowledgebase labeled "High Chill Apples." Another knowledgebase may contain the rule

"If latitude is above 40 degrees north,
then apply the rules in the High Chill Apples knowledgebase."

The knowledgebase containing this new rule would then be said to contain meta-knowledge (knowledge about when to apply or how to derive other knowledge).

Rule-Based Systems

The general principles that expert systems use to make decisions are often expressed in the form of *IF-THEN rules.* Rules are ordinarily divided into two segments. The IF segments of a rule are known collectively as the *left-hand side (LHS)* and individually as *premises, situations, conditions,* or *antecedents.* The THEN segments are known collectively as the *right-hand side (RHS)* and individually as *conclusions, actions,* or *results.* For example,

————LHS————
IF W is true (premise)
and X is true (premise)

————RHS————
THEN Y is true (conclusion)
and Z is true (conclusion)

In a rule, four types of logical choices are most common: *supposition* (IF X is true, THEN Z), *conjunction* (IF X AND Y are true, THEN Z), *negation* (IF X is NOT true, THEN Z), and *disjunction* (IF X OR Y is true, THEN Z). (Chapter 7 includes examples of these four types of choices.)

In some systems, rules are used only to describe allowances and limitations. That is, the rules detail what will be allowed to pass by the expert system's "censor" and what will not. Such rules are used to filter data as they pass through the expert system and are especially common in selection and configuration systems. These types of rules are known as *constraints.* Common constraints include *requisition* (IF you have this, THEN you MUST have that), *exclusion* (IF you have this, THEN you CANNOT have that), *implication* (IF you have this, THEN you SHOULD also have that), *substitution* (IF you need this, THEN you MAY USE that instead), and *limitation* (IF you have this, THEN you cannot have MORE THAN X number of those).

Frame-Based Systems

Aside from the use of rules, the other usual method of decision making within an expert system is *inheritance*. Inheritance involves the passing of values between blocks of categorized data. The generic term for these blocks of data (similar to the records or relations in a database) is *frames*. Within an expert system there are two kinds of frames. Blocks of general data are called *classes*, and specific instances within those classes are called *objects*. For example,

Currencies
Effect of high currency value in world market:
Imports cheaper, exports more expensive

is a class frame because the information applies to all currencies. Whenever a nation's currency has a high value in the world market, its imports will become relatively cheaper and its exports more expensive. But

Yen
Current value:
$.0054

represents only one object in the class Currencies because it is a specific instance of the general class of all Currencies.

Inheritance involves passing data between frames (class to class, class to object, object to object, object to class). In the currency case here, each specific object (each type of currency) will inherit

Effect of high currency value in world market:
Imports cheaper, exports more expensive

from the general Currencies class, making it unnecessary to type into the system

Yen
Effect of high currency value in world market:
Imports cheaper, exports more expensive

Swiss franc
Effect of high currency value in world market:
Imports cheaper, exports more expensive

Canadian dollar
Effect of high currency value in world market:
Imports cheaper, exports more expensive

and so on.

Basis of Reasoning

Expert systems that employ inheritance as their principal means of decision making are usually referred to as *frame-based* or *object-oriented* systems. Those systems that rely on *heuristics* (rules) are called *rule-based* or *production* systems (a production is a rule). Systems whose rules or frames are used to describe limits and allowances are called *constraint-based* systems. *Case-based* systems (those that are not just simple data-matching programs) often use inductive reasoning methods to arrive at their results (not to be confused with CASE—Computer-aided software engineering—the automated creation or examination of computer code). Most expert systems, combine more than one reasoning method in the same program.

"How long does it take to build an expert system?"

The short answer to this question has always been, "As long as it takes to teach a person the task involved." If the task is the scheduling of petroleum-products through pipelines , and it requires a person new to the job one year before he or she can handle that task of scheduling the transmission of non-compressible liquids through a pipeline network, then the expert system should require one year to build. This is because (at least in a deductive expert system) the KE must learn the task well enough to be able to encode the experts' knowledge. So, the expert system will be built at roughly the same rate at which the KE can absorb and duplicate the experts' skills.

But, in large systems expanded over many years, the system grows as the needs of the organization grow. And such a system may never really be "finished." When new products are added to a price list, for example, new rules must be added to a product configuration expert system that puts new products together with the old ones. When new pharmaceuticals are developed, new rules of chemical reaction must be added to an expert system molecular modeler. These systems grow "in realtime." That is, after they have been encoded with all the past domain knowledge of the experts, they gain knowledge of new products at the same time the experts do. Such systems remain "unfinished" as long as knowledge or sophistication in the domain increases.

The following criteria are important for determining the success of an expert system:

- Does the expert system solve the problem it was designed to solve or exploit the opportunity it was designed to exploit?

- Is the system being used?

- Does the system relieve experts or users of some of the burden of their work or (in an inductive system) create useful knowledge?

- Does the system distribute knowledge more efficiently or more widely than was possible before?

- Does the system make (or save) money?

"Can an expert system become better than the experts of which it is a clone?"

Yes.

First, a well-designed, well-implemented expert system will capture the experience and wisdom of domain experts *at their best*. It will not be swayed by political expediency, become ill, or be distracted, as a human expert might be.

Second, building an expert system is not a one-shot, specs-first, get-it-right-the-first-time operation. Experts can correct their own less-than-ideal performances when they recognize their mistaken reasoning in the expert system. What the system eventually reproduces, then, is experts who have seen the results of their decision making in most situations and have corrected their improper responses.

Of course, it is entirely possible for an expert system to make mistakes in judgment if those mistakes are incorporated into the system's rulebase or framebase. But frequent testing and use of the system will expose faulty assumptions and logic. The prototyping process itself almost guarantees that a system will perform at the experts' optimal performance levels eventually.

Beyond that, the expert system does not forget (unless specifically made amnesiac by rule/frame removal). This trait may account for expert systems' superior performance in diagnostic tasks that require the ability to recall information learned years earlier and never accessed until the current situation (as in computer network crash/dump analysis).

Expert systems also do not experience lapses of attention, which may account for their use in bond/currency/commodity trading (not to

---

replace the experts, but to supplement them). A moment's distraction of an expert in that arena may result in lost opportunities in the millions of dollars.

An expert system's greater span of perception (being able to keep more factors in mind at one time than a human can) has contributed to the success of expert systems in scheduling and configuration, tasks that involve remembering the current state of thousands of variables simultaneously and acting on unique combinations of those variables.

Finally, in large-scale industrial applications, the fact that more than one expert's experience can be incorporated into a system means that the expert system encompasses the skills—but not the limitations—of many talented people.

"I've heard a lot about expert systems being part of the 'Fifth Generation.' What were the other four generations?"

Hardware engineers often explain that computer design includes the following generations:

1. vacuum tube machines

2. transitorized machines

3. machines built using integrated circuits (chips)

4. very large scale integrated (VLSI) circuit machines

5. parallel processors

Fifth-generation parallel processing hardwares divide a computational task into segments and pass the segments to a series of processing units. All of the units act on the task simultaneously. And this division of labor improves performance while decreasing runtime.

The perspective of KEs, however, is different from that of hardware designers. "Generation" to a KE refers to the evolution of software, not hardware, over the last thirty years.

Machine code ($1s$ and $0s$—once the only way to provide instructions to a computer) is thought of as the first software generation.

Second-generation software refers to Assembly language, the lowest-level and perhaps most powerful computer language. It is the language in which system software (for example, operating systems and utilities) is most often written today.

The third generation of software includes all of the high-level languages from COBOL to Pascal to LISP (which is the second oldest high-level language still in use, after FORTRAN).

The fourth generation of software traditionally has meant 4GL program generators, software that allows the easy creation of reports and third-generation language source code. But fourth generation may now also refer to expert system development tools such as OPS5, Nexpert, or EPITOOL, which are written in high-level languages (in these cases, BLISS, C, and LISP, respectively).

The fifth generation of software is expert systems in all of their various forms.

Another generation of software, the sixth, denotes software for neural net systems, some artificial life systems, and software based on the principles of biological adaption and learning.

Each generation of software builds on the preceding one, as a programmer can see by tearing apart an expert system into its component languages. An expert system itself is part of the fifth generation, but the tool in which it was written is usually part of the fourth. And that development tool may be written in a third-generation language that itself is written in Assembler, which is only understandable to the central processing unit (CPU) because Assembler is written in first-generation machine code.

*"Could you explain some of the terminology used
by KEs, for example, 'certainty,' 'explanation
facilities,' and 'integration'?"*

Certainty and Fuzziness

In expert systems in which the entering data (from which the system must infer) are incomplete or imprecise, the use of *certainty factors* or *fuzzy logic* may be necessary.

Certainty factors are used when the likelihood of a particular premise or conclusion affecting a rule's results is less than 100%. (For example, "80% of the time, this premise is important." Or "In 7 out of the 10 past cases, this conclusion has resulted from this premise.") In such a situation, certainty factors can be used within the expert system to allow for shades of belief or probability. For instance, "If the furnace temperature is below 1200 degrees, there is a 0.8 (80%) likelihood of inadequate liquification (or, we can be 80% certain that inadequate liquification will occur)."

Expert systems that utilize knowledge that is not easily quantifiable may use some type of fuzzy logic. For example, when a user tells the system, "The flame in the oxyacetylene torch is 'very' blue," the system must ask supporting questions and build an internal scale of "blueness" to understand what the fuzzy concept "very blue" actually means. Such systems may use quantifiable thresholds to decide what is meant by both "very" and "blue" (for example, if the color is X% dark, then it is "very blue").

Even though certainty factors and fuzzy logic intuitively may seem useful in expert system design—because they address the problems of inexact and uncertain data—and even though they have been employed successfully in certain applications, commercial expert system developers often avoid them when their use is not demanded by genuinely incomplete data. In some cases, this avoidance is because *propagation of probability* is too sticky a problem. (For example, if the certainty of premise A is 0.3 and the certainty of premise B is 0.07, and the certainty of premise C is 0.24, how do those certainties interact to influence conclusion X? Should the expert system add the certainties together? Average them? Employ weighted averages? If so, how should weights be assigned? Why would one method of combining certainties be more valid than the others in a particular application? And what would "conclusion X has a 0.21609 certainty" mean?)

Also, the heuristic knowledge of domain experts, as practicing KEs have discovered, is rarely dependent on probabilities. Experts do not add weighted certainty factors in their heads to make decisions. So prodding an expert into coming up with a certainty factor of, say, 0.78 for a certain conclusion often leads to guessing and unnecessary obfuscation on the part of an expert who is forced to quantify for the KE what is not quantified in his or her own mind.

And also, the presence or absence of some kinds of data usually boosts certainty to 100%. Many knowledge engineers building commercial expert systems concentrate on finding those missing data (in expert interviews) rather than tinkering with incomplete data and certainty factors.

Explanation Facilities

In many expert systems, *explanation facilities* play an important role in explaining complex reasoning processes (for example, how decisions were made by the system). The most common of these explanation mechanisms is *justification.* Justification mechanisms peer back into an executed expert system to explain to a user how certain conclusions were reached. For example, a justifier in a computer-network security expert system might say:

Conclusion 68:[node 113 is penetrable] was reached
because the following premises were found to be true:

Premise 37:[predictable password used in system account]
Premise 39:[insufficient file protection on network information datafile].
These premises were invoked in Rule 98.

This kind of *backtracking* to provide explanations by justification
(not to be confused with backward chaining) can be used by an expert
system for purposes other than explaining reasoning. Backtracking can
also be employed by an inference engine to "unwind," or "uninvoke,"
rules (which have already fired) when a user changes his or her mind
(or, in many scheduling systems, when the system hits a deadend in its
planning). This ability of an expert system that allows users to modify
or retract previous responses is known as *non-monotonicity*. But because one rule can trigger another rule and that rule can ignite several
more (a process called *cascading*), non-monotonic systems can suffer
difficult *truth maintenance* problems. For example, rules which fired as
a result of old information may no longer be true given the user's new
or changed information. And those old rules have to be identified and
reset before the new information can be installed and acted upon by
the expert system.

Integration

When an expert system development project becomes large enough, it
may begin to branch out. It may become an *integrated* system, that is,
an expert system joined onto existing conventional programs. Or it may
become a *hybrid*, an expert system with conventional abilities built onto
it. The most common type of hybrid system handles both complex
calculations and symbolic manipulation, combining data processing or
scientific programming with artificial intelligence (AI). Many financial
expert systems are hybrid systems of this type. ("Hybrid" may also refer
to an expert system development tool that uses more than one knowledge representation scheme.)

An expert system linked to other expert systems, instead of to
conventional systems, creates a *knowledge network*. Such linked expert
systems are often tied to each other by means of intermediary files
known as *blackboards,* which the separate expert systems write to and
read from. (Blackboards are also used internally in a single expert
system.) A blackboard allows on-demand information exchange between the different parts of an expert system or between different expert
systems in a knowledge network. It provides a nexus through which the
systems communicate with each other, by writing onto the blackboard
when they have data or reading from the blackboard when they need
data.

*"Why can't I write my expert systems in COBOL. I already have
a large staff of fluent programmers, years of in-house
experience with the language, and a substantial investment in
hardware and software. Why do I need an expert system
development tool or language?"*

In truth, the only requirement of a language for it to be used for expert system development is a conditional predicate, an IF command. Since every computer language has an IF or an implied IF, it is technically possible to build an expert system in *any* language. The reason this is usually thought to be unreasonable is because each language has its own strengths and weaknessess. And the weaknesses of certain languages make rule-based or frame-based programming difficult.

Trajectory calculations, for example, are not done in COBOL because FORTRAN is more adept at handling complex number crunching. Programming is not taught to grade school students in COBOL because BASIC and other languages provide a syntax and vocabulary better suited to pedagogy. List- and report-making functions (such as payroll processing) are not done in PROLOG or LISP because COBOL provides more advantages for the programming and formatting of standard business applications. And expert systems are seldom built in COBOL because AI languages and tools are more deft in their manipulation of rules, frames, logic, and the other knowledge representation schemes and inference methods employed by expert systems.

"How does an expert system's performance improve?"

Users in organizations just beginning to investigate commercial AI sometimes expect that all expert systems will accomplish the following:

- improve their own performance automatically with practice
- learn from their own mistakes
- perform tasks no human being has yet been able to do

In fact, the type of system most likely to be implemented first in an organization is rule-based and deductive. And such systems do *not* automatically learn from experience or from past cases of successful problem solution. Their initial knowledgebase is built by tapping existing knowledge, not by creating new knowledge about tasks currently impossible for humans. And the purpose of such systems is not to discover new ways of accomplishing a task, but to make scarce expertise in that task more widely available.

The accuracy and validity of such systems generally *do* improve over time—but not because the expert system learns. The system's performance improves because KEs, experts, and users identify weaknesses in the knowledgebase and correct them by hand. Improvement in an expert system's performance, then, is generally the result of the prototyping process.

Not all expert systems are deductive, though. And the way in which an expert system's performance improves does depend upon its method of inference.

"What is the practical difference between deduction and induction? When would I use one over the other?"

What are deduction and induction?

From an academic viewpoint, deduction is nothing more than the drawing of conclusions from premises, which is what each rule in a rule-based system does. For example, the truth of Z will be deduced in the following rule (given that X and Y are true):

```
IF X is true
AND Y is true
THEN Z is true.
```

From a broader perspective, deduction has to do with applying general principles to solve specific problems. Induction has to do with studying specific problems in order to create those general principles.

For example, when Sherlock Holmes sees a man with a red tattoo of the word "kluge," he asks the man where he received the tattoo. The reply is "Nepal." He asks another man with the same tattoo and gets the same response. He eventually asks a hundred men the same question and is always told "Nepal." From these many specific cases he *induces* the general principle: "If someone has a red 'kluge' tattoo, then they have been to Nepal."

Armed with this general rule, Sherlock meets a man with the special tattoo. Without speaking to the man, he *deduces* (by applying his rule) that *this particular fellow*, whom he has never seen before, has been to Nepal. Elementary, what?

When are such systems built?

The glib saying "You can't build an expert system without an expert" is incorrect. A KE certainly can build an expert system without an expert. But the system cannot be deductive.

Deductive systems are built *when domain knowledge exists* and can be "cloned" into an expert system. Experts are usually debriefed and their knowledge incorporated into the knowledgebase of a deductive system. But inductive systems ordinarily are built when *only data,* not experts, exist. The data may be on the past performance of a particular piece of machinery, past real estate sales in a certain city, or past loads on the trunks in a telecommunications network.

The classic example of a commercial inductive expert system is the stock market analyzer. Brokerage houses and other financial institutions fill vast databases with market data that record the price of each stock during each minute of every day for the last one hundred years. But experts (technical, fundamental, quantitative, and qualitative analysts) often have difficulty prizing sensible patterns out of this overwhelming mass of data. An expert system, which sifts through the billions of bits of historical data (past cases) searching for patterns and creating rules or making recommendations for a day's trading based on what it has found, can be of great value. And such a system is inductive, not deductive.

How are deductive and inductive systems maintained and corrected?

In general, deductive systems improve when rules and/or frames are added, modified, or deleted from a knowledgebase by a KE in consultation with an expert. The deductive expert system's accuracy depends on the accuracy of its rules. And the system improves via a process of repeated testing, fine-tuning, and rule modification.

Inductive systems, on the other hand, induce rules from all the information they have at hand. The more cases (examples) they have to draw on—and the more detailed those cases are—the more specific and accurate the rules generated from them can be. So the validity of an inductive system's responses will usually improve in the following instances:

- when more relevant cases are added to the *training set* (the group of cases to be induced from)

- when more types of relevant data (more attributes) are added to the cases already in the training set (also called the *casebase*)

- when rules created by induction are "rogued out" of the created rulebase by hand—an extremely difficult process—(unless the rules are contrary to common sense and glaringly obvious) since the rules that inductive systems create are usually in fields of inquiry in which there are no experts capable of checking the validity of the rules without specifically testing them.

Correction, in fact, is an important problem for inductive systems because inductive systems can create rules that seem plausible to the expert system but that are quite wrong. This can happen when the system is forced to induce from incomplete information (for example, the system knows about only three types of birds—ostriches, kiwis, and penguins—and creates a rule based on these data stating that birds do *not* fly). Or the system may confuse contiguity with causality and become *superstitious*. That is, it may infer that one element in a situation influences another when, in fact, it doesn't (for example, the system, which knows the precipitation levels and populations of two cities—Seattle, Washington, and Carefree, Arizona—creates an erroneous rule stating that the amount of precipitation in any city is directly related to population size: the larger the city, the more rain). So, rules created by inductive systems have to be understood in this context and treated as likely to be true, but not necessarily true.

Deductive systems, of course, may also infer incorrectly, but those faulty inferences can be removed or changed more easily (when the expert sees them being inferred during testing of the system and points them out).

"What is the difference between backward and forward chaining? When would I use one rather than the other?"

Forward and backward chaining are control strategies: methods of directing the way in which a deductive expert system collects data.

Imagine the knowledgebase of an expert system as a net made of dozens of knotted fibers, a net stretched out on the ground in front of the expert system. The system will walk on the net, stepping from knot to knot, collecting data at each knot it treads on. Those data will influence its decision on which knot to go to next (not all knots need be trodden on).

A forward chaining system will begin at a knot, discover the data for that knot, and then move on to the next appropriate knot (based on the data already collected). Eventually, after the system has gathered enough data (has gone as far as it can go on the net), it will reach a conclusion (a hypothesis) and will explain to the user what it has inferred from the data it collected at each of the knots. Such a system is also called *data driven* because the data it collects drives the system in the direction of a certain conclusion.

A backward chaining system, on the other hand, will discover data that leads it to suspect a certain conclusion and will jump directly onto that knot (jump to a conclusion). Then the system will look back to see what kind of data it will have to collect (which knots behind it it will have to step on) to prove its supposed conclusion valid. (In a rule-based system, this often means that the expert system assumes a *conclusion* on the right-hand side of a rule is valid and then asks questions about the *premises* on the left-hand side to prove the conclusion true.) Such a system is also called *goal driven* because it posits a goal first (a hypothesis) and then tries to collect data to support that goal.

A hospital preadmissions diagnostic expert system uses this kind of backward chaining when interviewing a patient. It asks the patient what the trouble is. Then it quickly makes an assumption about possible causes based on the patient's answer. If the patient says, "My hand hurts," the system may immediately assume "blunt trauma" and then request examination of the hand. It may ask if the hand was slammed in a car door or used to play handball recently. "Blunt trauma" becomes the hypothesis, and the system asks subsequent questions to try to prove that hypothesis. During the course of the session, each hypothesis the system makes is verified or supplanted until a final cause for the problem is isolated.

By contrast, a system to put together custom-designed individual-corporation telecommunication networks employs forward chaining. It has to glean a good deal of information about the corporation's needs and phone uses before it can begin to configure the telecommunication network. So the system asks questions, gathers data, and—only after having collected all the data it needs—suggests an appropriate configuration.

Such an expert system could be written as a backward chainer, but it would incur a considerable amount of overhead by making assumptions as to how the network should be built, configuring those new networks, and then changing its assumptions and reconfiguring the network after new data had come to light.

For example, if the system asked, "How many long-distance calls do you make daily?" and configured a network based entirely on those data (made a hypothesis about what the customer needed and acted according to that hypothesis), such a configuration probably would have to be revised drastically after the answer to the next necessary question, "What is your annual budget for telecommunications?" because the original network design was too expensive. The system would have to change the network configuration again after the answer to "How many people will each secretary support?", again after "Which phones will require conference calling abilities?", and again after "Which phones will allow long-distance calls outside the country?" Under these circumstances, it makes more sense for the system to forward chain: to ask all the questions first and return a recommended configuration after all the requisite data have been gathered and the system has run out of relevant questions to ask.

During the design of an expert system, a clue as to whether it should forward or backward chain can sometimes come from the paradigm the system will work in. What the hospital preadmissions expert system does, for example, is diagnosis. And diagnostic applications are often backward chaining because they require the system to focus on the cause of a problem (make a hypothesis) quickly. If that proposed cause turns out to be false, the system will not have wasted too much effort and CPU time in assuming the hypothesis (or in changing its mind later). Most configuration and scheduling systems, however, are forward chainers (as is the telecommunications network designer) because the cost of proposing solutions (hypotheses) and then following through on those proposed solutions (actually reconfiguring the complex network every time the system gathers more data and changes its hypotheses) is too great.

Forward and backward chaining can be used together. In fact, most commercial expert systems commingle both strategies. They sometimes forward chain to reach a particular hypothesis and then backward chain to try to ensure that that hypothesis is true. And they may toggle repeatedly between control strategies until a final conclusion is reached.

An expert system that diagnoses open circuit defects in stereo receivers, for example, may forward chain to determine where the problem lies in the receiver—until it strikes a likely cause of the trouble. Then it backward chains to try to prove that the proposed cause is the correct one. Such a system would forward chain, trolling for a possible cause, this way:

"Does the power supply lamp light up?" **YES.**
(So the power supply is probably not the problem.)

"When the power supply is switched on, is there a thump in both speakers?" **YES.**
(So the power amp is probably not the problem.)

"Is there a hiss in both speakers and does the level of hiss change when the volume and tone (treble, bass) controls are turned up?" **YES.**

(So the pre-amp is probably not the problem.)

"When a tape system is played, can it be heard in both channels?" **YES.**

(So the tape is probably not the problem.)

"Is there a scratchy noise in the speakers when the source/input selector knob (AM, FM, tape, turntable) is turned?" **YES.**
(So the selector is probably not the problem.)

"Is the FM stereo indicator lamp on, and is there a stereo effect in both speakers?" **YES.**
(So the FM radio is probably not the problem.)

"Does the AM radio also work?" **NO.**
(This suggests an open circuit [broken wire] near the AM radio selector, and this becomes the hypothesis the system tries to prove.)

The system then begins to backward chain, trying to prove its assumption:

"Hypothesis: Open circuit near AM radio.
Does the meter react when the AM radio tuning knob (channel selector) is turned?" **YES.**
(This suggests that the defect does not lie somewhere beyond the AM radio, supporting evidence for its hypothesis.)

"Hypothesis: Open circuit near AM radio.
If one end of a clip lead (a wire) is connected to the AM radio detector and the other end to the source/input selector, does the AM radio work?" **YES.**
(Bingo. Conclusive evidence for the hypothesis.)

"All evidence points to an open circuit between the AM radio detector and the source/input selector as the cause of the problem."

Prospecting 3

The Knowledge Engineer as Systems Analyst

Prospecting is the process of discovering problems amenable to solution by an expert system. But it is also the process of finding new opportunities suitable for expert system exploitation. As a result, prospecting has two goals in every organization, one immediate and one distant. And the prospector's task is to study an organization from both points of view with an eye toward designing short-term and long-range expert system strategies.

Prospecting can be approached from the perspective of an entire organization, a single division, or a single job function. And it can be undertaken in three stages: diagnosis, analysis, and configuration. Diagnosis is the task of examining an organization's present and future problems and identifying areas that may be responsive to expert system solution. Analysis is the job of deciding whether an expert system will be a suitable solution to the problems identified, given the constraints of the domain and the organization. And configuration is the act of discerning the effects an expert system will have on the organization.

Diagnosis

The Users' Dissatisfaction List

Ferreting out application possibilities may begin with an interview of employees who are unhappy with the method they are currently using.

They may already have a written list of complaints. Or they may be able to list aloud the problems inherent in their present situation. In either case, from their litany of the shortcomings of the current system, a KE can deduce

- the specific system, task, or problem area to be scrutinized

- how the system should work ideally

- situations under which the current system fails

- the type of loss incurred as a result of the system's failure, such as
  - personnel time/energy
  - unnecessary hardware/software purchase/usage
  - lost opportunity for profit
  - high error ratios
  - customer dissatisfaction
  - inordinately high accounts receivable
  - lowered productivity

- the consequences and costs of leaving the situation unresolved

- previously attempted solutions to the problem and their relative successes

- suggestions to improve the current system

In this context, the "current system" may be an unsatisfactory manual process (such as recording information in log books for later perusal by a domain expert). It may be a non-productive conventional programming solution (such as a database that can be interpreted only by a domain expert). Or it may be an ineffective attempt to solve a problem via traditional methods (such as investing substantial resources in training personnel for a high-turnover job).

Whatever the original problem, user disaffection may be the cue for investigation by a prospecting knowledge engineer. And a specific user complaint may be the finger pointing to an expert system solution. In fact, criticism of a current system may provide a prospector with insight into larger-scale problems within the organization that become noticeable only at the user level. So, far from avoiding hostile users, a KE may actually wish to begin the prospecting task by exploring the reasons for user dissatisfaction and by seeking expert system solutions at that level.

The Managers' Wish List

A manager's wish list may offer the KE an opportunity to view the organization from the top down, to detect strategic openings, and to use expert systems to address future organizational, business, and technical needs within the group. From the manager's written or verbal wish list, a KE may be able to discern

- opportunities for expansion, including systems not feasible using other technologies (for example, "If only we could....")

- the benefits to be accrued from successful exploitation of the new area, such as

  - time savings
  - expertise applied evenly throughout an organization
  - new opportunities for profit
  - reduced error ratios
  - increased customer satisfaction
  - more rapid throughput
  - new customer services
  - greater productivity

- the consequences and costs of not exploiting the new opportunities

- ideas on how to explore and exploit the new field

- particular systems and tasks that have never quite yielded their full potential benefit to the organization

- how those systems should work ideally

In this environment, "strategic openings" may refer to a manager's attempt to anticipate future problems (such as retiring domain experts). It may relate to the creation of new products (such as fee-for-service advisory expert systems used directly by customers). Or it may have to do with long-range planning for the organization itself (such as using expert systems to forestall a skilled-personnel shortage in a particular domain).

Whatever its meaning in the specific organization, strategic top-down prospecting may yield greater results over the long term than any attempt at immediate problem solution. And, because of the development time and costs for even intermediate-sized expert systems, a longer-term approach to expert system creation may often be the most valid from both a business and an organizational standpoint.

The goal of the diagnostic phase of prospecting is to understand where expert systems could

- ameliorate long-standing problems

- eliminate bottlenecks

- exploit new opportunities

- facilitate existing processes
- increase productivity in particular job functions

One of the side effects of the diagnostic stage (part of the "beneficial residue" of the prospecting process) is the KE's newfound understanding of the organization's needs, objectives, and long-range strategy. The diagnostic report, delivered on completion of prospecting's first stage, may offer management the most complete up-to-date explanation of the organization's internal structure and future needs. And only after completion of the diagnosis can the analysis and prioritization of potential expert system applications begin.

Analysis

A prospector's principal assignment is always to ascertain the true nature of a problem. What seems, at first glance, to be a matter of scarce expertise may actually be the result of in-house political feuding that prohibits domain experts from applying their expertise where it is needed. Similarly, what appears to be an employee productivity problem may, in fact, be one of faulty communication between labor and management. And, occasionally, a task that looks to be a prime candidate for an expert system may be dealt with more easily through the creation of a user manual or a simple database.

In the first case, an ombudsman may be needed to resolve the political squabbling. In the second, the establishment of regular informational meetings might improve group communication. In the third situation, production of educational materials or an on-line data repository could be the answer. But none of these scenarios would call for the talents of a KE.

In fact, the analysis stage of prospecting is often largely a matter of culling a few legitimate expert systems from a large pool of prospective applications. To aid in this selection process, a KE may ask a series of questions aimed at filtering acceptable systems from the list of possibilities.

Exclusionary Questions

Any one of the following factors may contravene the development of the expert system.

Q   Can this task be accomplished using available software?

A   If an off-the-shelf package for general ledger, word processing, or database inquiry can solve the problem, there is no reason to build

---

an expert system. Both cost and development time considerations will mitigate against the construction of an expert system if a simpler alternative is available.

Q Can the task be accomplished using standard data processing practices?

A *Least-cost solutions are always preferable. If the problem is one of inefficient use of present resources, then elimination of code redundancy, reorganization of the database, or restructuring of the organization may be the answer. By remaining within the realm of conventional methodology, expert system training, hardware, software, and development costs will be saved to solve problems that cannot be solved efficiently by ordinary methods.*

Q Can the task be accomplished solely by algorithm, formula, or equation?

A *Valid algorithmic approaches include standard risk/benefit analysis, econometric modeling, simulation, statistical analysis, and spreadsheet data manipulation. Valid non-algorithmic approaches include all heuristic-based (rule-based, frame-based, object-based) methods. If an equation or a decision support model alone can achieve the desired results, it will be the more suitable approach.*

Q Does a domain expert exist (for a deductive system), and is the expert willing to participate?

A *A deductive expert system will not be able to solve any problem in an area in which no experts are available. Deductive expert systems can clone, codify, and distribute scarce knowledge, but they cannot create it. (If no experts exist for a particular task, an inductive system may have to be built.)*

No employee who gains prestige by doing a certain job will be likely to assist in the development of a system that reduces that prestige. Arbitrageurs, for example, are notoriously unwilling/unable to cooperate in the development of systems that may supplant them.

Q Will management cooperate?

A *Managers whose status and financial compensation depend on the number of their subordinates surely will have no incentive to reduce their headcounts in favor of expert systems. This is one reason that advisory expert systems are far more common than systems that*

*completely obsolesce a domain expert. Advisory systems aid an
expert in the performance of a job, but usually do not remove the
need for the human expert.*

Q Is this a problem suitable to solution by an expert system, or should
it more appropriately be solved using another form of technology?

A *Sometimes establishing a local area network, an electronic mail
system, or a multi-windowing/multi-tasking environment will be the
better use of limited funds. Ideally any problem should be resolved
using already available tools. When this is not possible, least-cost
and least-technical purchases are generally preferable. Only when
the problem is of a type or size that makes other approaches
unworkable or insufficient should an expert system be proposed.*

Q If there are other experts in the domain, but they do not do as well
as one particular expert, can that expert's skills be transferred?

A *Maybe. For example, if experts in other manufacturing plants just
don't know how to apply the best expert's methods, then an expert
system that applies those techniques and interprets the results may
be useful to everyone doing that job. But if the other experts have
tried those methods and have discovered that they don't work
anywhere but under the best expert's specific plant conditions, then
the best expert's skills may not be transferable to other plants. And
building an expert system may not solve anyone's problems.*

Practical Financial Questions

Q Would it be less costly (in the long term) simply to train more people
to perform the job or to compile the knowledge into a handbook?

A *Matrices, such as the "table of bad-check laws by state," may be all
that is required to open up an organization's knowledge bottleneck.
Scribbled notes compiled by an experienced user over years of
on-the-job training and published in a memo may be all that is
necessary to solve a problem in user education. And a conventional
training program offered by external consultants or a human
resources department may resolve long-standing difficulties in
maintaining a highly skilled workforce or managerial staff.*

*Expert systems certainly have their uses. But they should be viewed
only as one more arrow in an organization's quiver, rather than as
the cannonball that will knock down all walls to success.*

Q Could the expert system's development costs be amortized over a long period of usage? Will the knowledgebase's volatility (the rate at which knowledge in the domain changes) allow that?

A *Even if the cost of constructing an expert system appears untenable on the surface, amortization may make it not only acceptable but desirable. The costs of training personnel in high-volume/ high-turnover fields generally remain stable or increase over time. But the costs of a tutorial expert system, once developed, should be minimal and should not increase over time if the domain's knowledge does not change. That consideration may make the expert system the solution of choice over the long haul. But if the expert system will be training few people, training people for only a short period, or working in a field with highly volatile knowledge, then the system may not justify its development costs.*

For example, the cost of building a computer tutor for training new underwriters or machine tool operators might be distributed over hundreds of sessions and dozens of pupils. And its development might not only reduce the need for human trainers but also allow a company's policies to be promulgated to all trainees equally. However, if the number of people to be trained is small and the attrition rate low, the optimal solution may be standard classroom education.

Q Could development costs be recouped in a few successful transactions?

A *Occasionally, a business manager may expect to recover the costs of developing an expert system with only a few highly profitable executions. Expert systems that monitor and report on detected faults or opportunities often fall into this category. A foreign currency trading system, for example, that uses both algorithmic and heuristic cues (a hybrid system) to recognize technical analysis chart patterns and then detect when those patterns have been breached (breakouts) could pay for itself in one transaction, even when used as an adviser or "second guesser" by human traders. A legal document analysis/configuration system that examines legal contracts for inconsistencies (unintended liability or unintended breach of contract) could pay for its development with the discovery of one important omission/commission.*

It is the task of the prospecting KE to ascertain whether an expert system can, in fact, pay for its own construction with only a few anomaly detections, especially if that is the system's sole cost justification.

Q Over what time frame will the expert system's perceived benefits justify its development, implementation, and maintenance costs?

A *Commercial-grade expert systems require time to construct, test, and modify. So in any project in which a prompt solution is mandatory, expert systems seldom will be the answer. For example, a process control expert system designed to schedule operations in a major steel mill soon to be replaced by mini-mills will probably not be cost justifiable, given the system's limited opportunity for usage. Part of the prospecting KE's job at this stage is to determine the time windows for the contemplated systems' development. Only then can cost justification and project selection begin in earnest.*

Q Can the expert system be constructed in tiers, levels, or stages that would allow the delivery of a lower-level expert system before the entire project is completed, thereby effectively using the finished part of the expert system to help pay for the entire system's development?

A *Anyone providing the funding for an expert system would like to see results within memory of the decision to build the system. An expert system requiring five years of development before a single real-world test of its power can be made will be difficult to justify. And very few commercial expert systems are funded as long-term research projects. So the ideal expert system should begin to pay for its own development as soon as possible.*

One method of accelerating the usefulness of a system is to build it in layers, each of which can be utilized separately in some part of the organization. Such an approach, when possible, means that prototypes are occasionally "frozen" and distributed to users, not for testing but for actual use. And it may mean that the early finished layers will pay for future development and refinement of the entire system.

Q Are the experts expert by virtue of their special knowledge or because they have access to tools that other people don't have?

A *Occasionally experts will be the best at a particular job only because they have access to more information or better tools. In such a case, it would make no sense to devise an expert system. Just distributing the special technique or information to others would help them improve their performance. So, discovering precisely what tools (spreadsheet programs, historical usage data, special formulas, specific information) experts are using in their jobs and determining whether those same tools are available to others doing the same job may make the decision of whether to build an expert system easier.*

Only when an expert has the same information and tools as others doing the same job, but uses that information and technology more skillfully can an expert system be considered.

Q Will this project involve integration?

A *Integration (interfacing with existing conventional programs, databases, other expert systems, or hardwares) may add considerable time to the final implementation date of an expert system. It also may require technical sophistication in a variety of fields—DP, MIS, data communications, blackboard architectures (the use of intermediary files between disparate systems), or hardware setup and maintenance. So any project involving integration will require more initial time spent on team building and consensus building among all of the system builders before the overall system can be constructed.*

Another consideration is that the expert system that is linked to other programs may be at the mercy of those other constituent parts. For example, an expert system that requires input from a database to function will have to wait for a linkage to the database before becoming usable. Such complications add time and costs to a project.

Q Are the necessary tools available?

A *Expert systems are written using languages or tools that may not be available on all hardwares. Matching the needs of users (backward chaining, frame-based representation, icon-based menus, integration, sophisticated knowledge modeling) with the tools available should be started early in the system development process.*

Q Has some domain knowledge already been codified?

A *Knowledge acquisition can be a lengthy process. If the schedules of domain experts are tight, knowledge elicitation can be a difficult operation. Therefore, any knowledge that is already formalized or documented may be of help in building the expert system and can greatly facilitate the system's early development. Manuals, informal notes compiled by users or the domain expert, handbooks, college texts on the subject, memos, and visual aids created by domain experts or users can all provide encodable information. With such codified expertise, a KE can sometimes create an initial expert system prototype even before the first interview with a domain expert, saving knowledge acquisition time and money.*

Configuration

Once the problem has been explored and possible applications filtered, what remains is determining the effect an expert system will have on the organization. This may mean assessing the impact of the expert system on its potential users. Or it may involve determining how the new system will be influenced by the existing electronic (DP/MIS/DSS) environment. Or it may mean understanding the organizational politics that might affect how (or even whether) the expert system is used. In short, it requires thinking in terms of who, how, and where—all factors that will influence the eventual success of the project.

At this stage, the following questions should be considered:

Q Will the experts have time to participate in the project?

A *The reason most expert systems are built is because domain experts in an organization are scarce and overworked. Although an expert system will eventually lighten the experts' load, it often will require those experts to add knowledge acquisition sessions to their already full schedules for many months.*

In some professions, such as foreign currency trading, the experts are too valuable to be called away even to contribute to the system's development. In such cases, experts emeritus (floor managers) or sub-experts (backroom analysts) may become the system's contributors. But, in those cases, the expert system's role in an organization will usually change from expert replacement to expert support or supplementation.

Q What are the scheduling and location constraints of the parties involved?

A *If the experts are in Chicago, the KEs in Boston, the management in Atlanta, and the users in plants scattered across the U.S., arranging interviews and demonstrations may take some juggling of schedules, and that may add to the cost of a system.*

There is no reason for this kind of long-distance, multiple-site project not to be undertaken if other factors favor it. But it is likely to be more expensive than a one-site-contains-all system.

Q Will the expert system require the knowledge of more than a single domain expert?

A *Contrary to expectation, gathering knowledge from more than one expert seldom involves the problem of conflicting opinion, since experts working in the same organization generally defer to each other when the KE's questions concern one or the other expert's specialty. Experts who are motivated to download some of their work onto the expert system will rarely waste time in squabbling with their fellow gurus.*

But conflicting schedules may become a problem, preventing more than one expert from appearing in a room for knowledge acquisition at the same time. And that may slow the pace of acquisition if the KE wants all the experts involved to view the prototype at each step in its evolution.

Q What are the expectations of each of the parties involved in the project?

A *"Expectations management" is always a part of expert system development. Although specifications may be loose, especially at the start of a project, goals should be clearly understood by all parties involved. Goals are best divided into short-term, intermediate-term, and long-term and spelled out for the individual participants (for example, how much of the system the users will have access to at which point in development) to keep expectations under control.*

Q Will the expert system be used?

A *In a commercial setting, there is little use in building systems that will not be used to generate revenue or contain costs. So, user involvement and acceptance of the system from its inception are crucial.*

Summary

Prospecting is the task of identifying and prioritizing prospective expert system applications. It involves three stages of discrimination. The first, diagnosis, allows a KE to discern where the organization's problems and opportunities lie. The second, analysis, involves the selection of applications suitable for expert system development. And the third, configuration, entails evaluating the impact of the system on the organization. At any stage of this process, a potential application may be dropped entirely from consideration.

A KE should keep the following checklist in mind in determining the advisability of developing an expert system:

- Is an off-the-shelf package available?
- Are standard data processing practices useful?
- Are algorithms, formulas, or equations useful?
- Is the domain expert willing?
- Is management cooperative?
- Is another technology more appropriate?
- Are the expert's skills transferrable?
- Is training or a handbook better?
- Can the costs be amortized, or will a few transactions recoup costs?
- Does the development time frame justify building a system?
- Are tiers, levels, and stages of construction possible?
- Is integration involved?
- Are the necessary tools available?
- Is some knowledge already codified?
- Is the domain expert's schedule amenable?
- Are the location/travel costs acceptable?
- Is there more than one expert?
- Is MIS/DP cooperative?
- Are the expectations of the team members set?
- Is there any prestige loss among project participants?
- Are any users or experts unhappy about displacement?
- Will users use the system?

Because problem cases are often more instructive than situations in which everything goes right, the following actual case of a prospecting interview and analysis is presented. It illustrates that even projects with strong management support can be entirely unacceptable from a knowledge engineering standpoint.

Domain: Financial services

Project Task: Block equity trading for a brokerage house

Paradigm: Analysis/interpretation/prediction/diagnosis

Purpose: Advisory/consultancy

Background

We are meeting with a vice president and a senior systems analyst for the brokerage house trading floor (a brokerage house buys and sells stock for itself and for its clients). We are discussing possible applications in block equity trading and hedging (a block is a large lot of stock, typically 10,000 shares).

What We Know from Homework Done Before Coming to This Meeting

Bond, equity, and commodity (including foreign exchange) dealers generate substantial revenues for financial institutions around the world. They also command impressive salaries for their skills in

- market analysis

- arbitrage

- hedging

Market analysis is the prediction of future movements in price and influences the timing of trading purchases (for example, judging the validity of implied-forward-rate calculations before the purchasing of short term government bonds).

Arbitrage is the simultaneous buying and selling of the same item in two different markets to take advantage of the price differential (for example, buying 10 million ounces of silver in Tokyo at $6.02/ounce and selling them simultaneously in New York at $6.04/ounce).

Hedging is the protection of gains and the reduction of risk in financial transactions by the astute purchase of instruments, securities,

---

and/or contracts that will rise when one's own major deals fall (for example, buying a representative stock put-option (which will become more valuable when the value of the stock falls) to hedge a portfolio of recent block equity buys).

The Vice President Speaks

"We would like to build an expert system to help our traders. What we want to know from you is whether such a system is possible. If it is, we'd like to know how we should begin building it and whether you see any problems that we haven't anticipated.

"We want a system that will advise block equity traders on

- whether to make a trade (1)

- when to make the trade (2)

- how to hedge the trade once they have made it (3)

"We also want the system to watch the deals the traders make and tell a trader if he has gone over his trading loss limit for the day, or if he has committed an obvious error such as ordering 1000 *blocks* of stock when he meant to purchase 1000 *shares* of the stock (4).

"We actually need 12 different expert systems: one for each trader, because each expert trades differently (5). And we need an expert system that will be sensitive to current market conditions, which we get from the feed over the wire (6).

"We don't want to create knowledgebases that will completely clone our traders (7). We want the knowledgebase to be somewhat erasable (8), so the traders won't think we are trying to replace them by putting their brains in a box (9).

"And we would like the entire project to begin on June 1 and end on December 22, just before the annual bonuses are given out (10).

"What do you think?"

What the Knowledge Engineer Hears in This Brief Interview

1. Part of the system will involve diagnosis: deciding whether conditions are right to trade.

2. Part of the system will involve scheduling: assessing when a trade should be executed.

3. Another part of the system will involve diagnosis: deciding which of several hedging options should be selected.

4. Part of the system will act as a monitor/watchdog: alerting traders to certain dangerous conditions (four different subsystems, so far, on which we could begin working).

5. There may be some similarities between traders, but 12 different systems will require a lot of time.

6. Warning! Sounds like an unbounded domain problem (see Chapter 10, "Common Problems"). Find out exactly what "current market conditions" means to the traders. Exactly which factors will have to be taken into consideration by the expert system? The effect of droughts in the Midwest on processed food stocks and the effect of student riots in South Korea on U.S. automobile stocks? Or only such factors as the release of consumer price information by the U.S. federal government? Degree of difficulty varies widely depending on the factors to be included in the finished system.

7. This remark suggests either bad experiences in the past or a thorough review of the AI literature. Both may be positive for this project.

8. Erasable knowledgebases are possible—within limits. This should be investigated further. Erase values only or attribute/properties as well? Or entire rules and frames? Does "erasable" actually mean that the traders should be able to change the importance of certain factors (say, the importance of higher unemployment figures)? Or does it mean that the trader essentially should be able to create his own knowledgebase from scratch every day (may not be possible)?

9. Has there been some resistance from the traders to AI already? Do they feel threatened? This would certainly place their participation in the project in jeopardy.

10. The entire project in six months? Not possible. The extensive amount of integration to existing conventional systems and livefeeds and the number of parts to the system would necessitate a longer time span.

This system was not built in the form in which it was originally requested.

For comparison, here is a prospecting scenario for a system that was found acceptable—and that was built.

Domain: Telecommunications

Project Task: A telecomm help desk advisory system

Paradigm: Diagnosis/analysis

Purpose: Advisory

Background

We are meeting with the director of MIS for a large telecommunications firm.

The Director Speaks

"We were hoping to design an advisory expert system that would assist our customer support people in dealing with the public (1). In the beginning, we would like a system that assists the support folks in their jobs. But in time, we would like to shift the system out into the field and even into the offices of our customers so they will have direct access to our expertise in the field (2) and so we can ease people out of the hotline job and into something more interesting for them (3).

"The job the hotline people do demands a lot of skill and experience, but it's not a very high-status or high-paying job. And we think that the people doing the job, who will act as the experts for the expert system, will be very cooperative. They would just as soon do something more interesting with their lives. And we would prefer to use their knowledge and competence in other areas of the company (4). But right now we can't afford to spare them to do other tasks, because it takes too long to train them in their job, and there are too few of them to go around. So they've become a very scarce resource (5).

"Help desk people sit by the phones all day and answer questions from our customers about our specific services. They might offer recommendations to our customers on the installation, auditing, or maintenance of certain kinds of lines, for example. We were hoping to use newly hired people and temporaries in this position. Until now, we've trained people—actually apprenticed them with an experienced person—for this job, but it takes a year for someone to get good. And then they either leave or are promoted (6).

"We were hoping the temporaries could diagnose customer problems using the expert system (7), and solve customers' problems over the phone by just reading the system's suggestions off the screen. They could read questions off the screen and into the phone, then type in answers given by the customer. Then the expert system could analyze the problems and offer solutions and explanations.

"We tried just having them look things up in manuals (8), but it takes forever to get back to the customer that way (9). And manuals don't

---

exist for all or even the most common problems. Also, new people usually don't know which manual to look in. So we thought an expert system would better serve our purposes (10).

"The help desk folks get about 200 calls a day (11). But the questions they get are all in only three or four different areas. We thought we could start with one area, maintenance problems, since those are the most important. And then, when we had some experience with that area, we'd move on to other areas (12).

"We're not under the gun as far as time is concerned, but we'd like to begin soon (13). What do you think?"

What the Knowledge Engineer Hears in This Brief Interview

1. A good start. Help desks generally are good expert system applications.

2. The system can be built in tiers and will be useful at each stage: use by help desk personnel, use by field support personnel, direct use by customers.

3. There does seem to be a concern shown for the experts and the users and their eventual fate when the system has been completed (and displaces the experts).

4. Not only is there no resistance from the experts in the development of a system to supplant them, they should, in fact, welcome the system's completion. There appears to be both a push from management and a pull from the experts to get this system built: the ideal political combination.

5. The distribution of scarce expertise is one reason for the system's creation.

6. Other methods of solving this problem—conventional training and manuals—have been tried but have not succeeded. That should strengthen the case for the construction of an expert system.

7. The user-interface must be self-explanatory for naive users.

8. Some of the knowledge we will need has already been codified. If the information in the manuals is still valid, we may be able to accelerate acquisition by decomposing manuals into the knowledgebase first.

9. An increase in response rate is another reason for the system's development.

10. The use of manuals would also seem to imply that the system may be able to be built as a standalone application. The amount of integration/hybridization involved will have to be investigated further. But this may actually be one of those rare standalone systems.

11. We can amortize the cost of construction over many customer calls successfully handled.

12. It will be possible to work on one segment of the larger system first and then use what we learn in building that fragment to add the other pieces.

13. No onerous time constraints.

Overall impression very favorable. Development of this system recommended.

Beginning a Project   **4**

The Knowledge Engineer as Groundbreaker

Experienced knowledge engineers employ certain rules of thumb when they begin a new project. The more important of these rules follow.

Realize that not all problems can (or should) be solved by an expert system.

When the manufacturing personnel in a company's factory do not get along with the design engineers and would like to clone the designers' abilities into an expert system so they can have access to the design knowledge without having to interact with the design engineers, that is a problem that expert systems *may* alleviate. But it is a problem that would be *better* solved through mediation with an ombudsman or through personnel changes. An expert system, in this case, would treat only one symptom of a larger problem, not the problem itself, and would therefore be inappropriate.

Be perceived as a giver, not a taker.

Be seen as someone who is bringing food to the table, rather than as one more hungry mouth to feed. The first sentence spoken to users, experts, and managers should be, "What can I do to help you?" (rather than "This is what I will need from you").

Be perceived as an additional resource at the disposal of users and managers, rather than as a drain on existing resources. Be seen as someone who will provide assistance, not require other people to sacrifice their time. And expend far more effort in considering the solution to the user/manager/expert's problem than in discussing AI.

If project participants are convinced that problem solution is the KE's goal (that he or she will be measured by how well the problem is solved, not by how well an expert system is inserted into the organization), then the KE will become the confederate of the users, managers, and experts. The KE will become one of the group, with everyone working to solve a common problem. If the project participants know that "their KE" is joining forces with them and that the KE will have as much to gain or lose as they will, then the expert system will be seen as a legitimate attempt to aid the group, not as just an excuse to build an expert system.

Provide information. Avoid hype and tripe.

If managers, users, and experts are curious about the application of expert systems in their domain, speak to their needs. Discussing shop floor process control systems with financial people will not work. And detailing foreign currency hedging systems to telecomm hardware engineers will serve little purpose. Above all, avoid using toy or game-playing programs to illustrate AI concepts. Chess playing and auto repair programs often trivialize expert systems in the minds of an audience considering the technology. Instead, ground presentations and demonstrations in the domain the audience will find important.

Understand the problem to be tackled before making major purchases of hardware, software, or consulting services.

Appropriate tools, inference mechanisms, knowledge representation schemes, hardware, paradigms, system architectures, and the duration and cost of a project will all be suggested by initial understanding of the problem. So, examine the task to be undertaken before investing in hardware, software, or fleshware. Not all tools will be of value. Not all hardwares will facilitate the development process. Not all training programs will be suitable. And the way to make a careful and profitable selection is to understand precisely what the tools, hardware, and consultants will need to do, something that can be determined only after

- the problem has been studied
- the skills and needs of the developers, managers, and users have been ascertained

- costs, benefits, training, portability, and compatibility have been analyzed

Shop around.

Expert system development is an economic decision. So take nothing on faith. Look at the applications that have been built using a particular tool or by a certain consultant on a given hardware. And compare them to the organization's needs and budget.

Determine the players.

Ascertain who the users, managers, developers, domain experts, and knowledge engineers will be for a particular project. List their names, titles, objectives, and definitions of success. (Sending the list to each participant is often a good idea. When people know their names will be widely associated with a project, they usually take more interest in it to protect their own reputations.)

Meet with each participant, if possible, in a location in which he or she will feel most comfortable. Begin to understand each participant's schedule and idiosyncracies.

Make the first prototype a standalone, rather than a hybrid or integrated system.

An independently functioning system (rather than one linked to existing programs or files) is the ideal first prototype. Integration requires a great deal of effort, effort that is initially better spent solving substantive issues within the expert system rather than dissipated in linkage entanglements.

A standalone allows the KE to focus on expert system matters before tackling linkage issues. It allows for rapid and significant changes to the knowledgebase without affecting other programs or databases. A standalone also minimizes disruption and inconvenience to employees operating under an existing system. It can be tested without changing the way things are done in a department at the moment. It allows for portability of the expert system, which can be developed and tested offsite. And it reduces the demand for the time and resources of MIS personnel who might assist in linking the expert system to databases or conventional programs.

Change no current policies, but get commitment.

Interfere as little as possible in the daily routine of the project participants. Whenever practical, work within the organization's current methods of operation. Disrupt and inconvenience as seldom as possible.

But before getting very far into the development cycle, be certain to have a commitment from each of the users, managers, and experts to participate in the system's development.

Offend no one.

Expert systems are not short-term projects. So, it's impossible to carry out slash-and-burn programming, trampling scorched users underfoot in the haste to reach a deadline. Development may be long and laborious. And anyone (MIS/DP staff, users, managers, domain experts, or KEs) may become the critical link in the system's completion. When funding is under discussion, anyone may become the crucial extoller or detractor of the expert system during reviews. So tread on no toes.

Research the domain.

If there is a book on the domain, read it. If there are background articles that may provide a feel for the field, seek them out.

A domain expert who knows the KE has made an effort to understand the area of expertise will always be more cooperative than one who is treated as an information cow to be milked.

Set appropriate expectations.

Set expectations with each group that will have contact with the expert system. If users expect automatic learning from a simple deductive system, they will be disappointed no matter how sophisticated and useful the system they are given is. Clarify at the start what will be attempted and what will be delivered.

Establish provisional goals and guidelines.

Determine what will be provided in the first draft of the expert system, in later versions, and in the final implementation (features, functionality, and flash). Decide which subproblems will be tackled initially. Mock-ups (screen facades and dummy data) may be of use at this stage.

Establish reasonable deadlines.

Short time frames (for example, within two weeks) are best at the start of a project, when people have the most enthusiasm and energy. At meetings, report on progress being made toward the final goal and on new features or functions available for the users to test. Aim for small (but not trivial) goals at first, then build those smaller accomplishments into a larger development plan.

Create the first prototypes quickly.

Showing even a tiny expert system to a new domain expert will clarify more in the expert's mind than several days of verbal explanation. Frequently, after days of briefings, lectures, and informal discussions, a new project participant will utter an "Ah-ha" of comprehension on seeing an expert system actually working for the first time. The most common comment during the presentation of a first prototype is, "Oh, I see what you mean now."

Use the following checklist.

- Capsule summary of problem to be addressed
- Expected functionality and features of expert system (at each stage of development)
- Hardware
- Software
- Domain expert
  - Principal needs
- Manager
  - Principal needs
- User
  - Principal needs
- Other interested parties
  - Principal needs
- Texts or manuals available
- Place of meetings
- Time of meetings
- Date (projected) of first prototype's completion

Domain: Telecommunications

Project Task: Network fault detection

Paradigm: Anomaly detection and monitoring

Purpose: Advisory/proxy

System to Be Built

An expert system will be built to assist troubleshooters in diagnosing problems which have occurred on a telecommunications network. The system will analyze, diagnose, and make solution recommendations after reviewing errors and failures noted by the alarm-detection system already installed.

In the First Meeting

1. Establish exactly who we will be dealing with
   a. Which groups will we work with for knowledge acquisition (domain expert) and testing (users)?
   b. Which group will accept the completed system?
   c. Who are the managers of those groups?
2. Set expectations about deliverables with all concerned parties
   a. functionality
   b. features
   c. flash
3. Suggest to managers, users, and experts what they can expect from the expert system.

General Functionality of the System

1. We will deliver a standalone expert system prototype within six months.
2. "Standalone" means that the expert system will request data from the user via the screen interface, rather than directly pulling the data from the network.

---

3. After the prototype has been completed (or during its development, if we have the funding),work will begin on making the integration linkages to the network to eliminate most of the user's role in data input.

4. The system will act in an advisory capacity to the human telecomm network troubleshooters.

5. The system will focus on data problems (rather than on phone or computer hardware/software problems).

6. The system will concentrate on handling a certain subset of the fault detection problem to begin with, but may also know something about other subsets.

7. The system will be built in such a way as to make expansion of the system simple, including

   - copious documentation in the knowledgebase of each rule, ruleblock, and frame, and, in the inference engine, of the engine's overall strucure and of each module within the whole structure
   - no use of acronyms for variable names
   - no coding of labyrinthine inheritance schemes or byzantine inference methods

8. The documentation is to be done toward the end of the cycle, before the six-month prototype is delivered, to allow for frequent additions, deletions, and modifications of code during the prototyping process.

9. The system will be built in such a way that its skeleton (inference engine) can be easily separated from its knowledgebase, so that the same skeleton can be used for other diagnostic projects inside the company, increasing the projected return on investment.

10. The system will be built in such a way as to minimize training requirements (goal: five minutes of training in how to use the expert system, that is, an expert system that is essentially self-explanatory).

General Features

1. The system will make general recommendations for action on problems it has identified after a few questions. It will make

more specific recommendations and give specific instructions for
action as the number of questions the system asks (the amount
of data it analyzes) increases.

2. The user will not have to ask many questions before the expert
   system offers some type of advice (backward chaining
   deduction). Ideally, some level of advice will be presented to the
   user after only the first question.

3. Advice will be in the form of an explanatory graphical
   representation (a color schema of the network, highlighting in
   red the areas in which faults are most likely to have occurred)
   and in simple English.

4. The amount of typing by the user will be kept to a minimum
   using arrow keys, light pens, pucks, and/or mice.

5. In a later implementation, the system will be autonomous,
   requiring no input from the user. It will derive its knowledge of
   the telecomm network directly from livefeeds detailing the
   network's disposition in realtime. It will filter alarms denoting
   network problems and focus its attention on the most significant
   problems in a given circumstance. It will offer to the
   troubleshooter on-screen

   - a ranked list of deduced problems from highest to lowest
     priority (based on severity and necessity of prompt response)
   - an interpretation of the meanings of network alarm signals
     which often arrive in large groups (an important feature in
     the event of, say, a cable cut, which may by itself result in
     several thousand different alarm/error messages appearing on
     the troubleshooter's screen at once)
   - suggestions for the solution of the problems it detects
   - a graphical display of network topography highlighting the
     problem sites
   - explanations of its recommendations for action

Suggested Benefits of This Expert System

1. Greater accuracy of diagnosis

2. Reduced error ratios

3. Quicker total problem response time in later phase of expert
   system development when the livefeed is instituted

4. Greater attention span of the expert system, resulting in catching of problems that slip by human experts

5. Detection of potential and incipient problems before those problems reach crisis level

What We Will Do Next

We will set the time for the initial knowledge acquisition session.

1. We will want to speak with the users' and the experts' managers to gather background information.

2. We will want to spend the bulk of our time garnering raw knowledge from people who actually do the work, along with an idea of what would help them in their job (so that they will use the system when we deliver the prototype).

Paradigms and Purposes   *5*

The Knowledge Engineer as Taxonomist

An expert system is generally classified by paradigm, purpose, and domain. Paradigm refers to the type of problem the expert system solves. Purpose is the reason behind the system's development. And domain refers to the field in which the expert system will operate.

The following brief guide describes the more common paradigms and purposes and their implications for the practicing KE.

Paradigms

Diagnosis/Classification

Diagnostic systems are traditionally used to perform at least one of the following tasks:

- determining whether a problem has occurred
- discovering what that problem is
- finding out what caused the problem
- ascertaining what will result from the problem's occurrence
- deciding how the problem can be fixed
- recommending solutions

Classification

Classification is often the first step in a diagnostic system, but it may be used on its own as well. Classification involves categorizing a problem (or an opportunity) given to the expert system according to one of the following areas:

- the problem's severity (the promptness with which it should be attended to)
- the "type" of problem (the general area in which the problem lies)
- where the problem is physically located in a large piece of machinery

Examples of diagnostic/classification systems include the following applications:

- *blast furnace trouble and inefficiency detection.* isolating the causes of furnace problems and inefficiencies that might result in the production of an inferior grade of steel or in the loss of production time

- *mortgage underwriting.* accepting/rejecting/advising on proposed loans based on such factors as credit history, purchase price, loan maturity, and down payment

- *telecommunications equipment troubleshooting.* testing and determining the causes of failure in a piece of equipment, such as a switching exchange, before that piece is built into a larger configuration of machinery already working in the field.

Knowledge Representation and Inference

Diagnostic systems are usually backward chaining because quick determination of a problem's cause (employing few questions) is often called for in such systems.

Rules in diagnostic systems may be used to infer causes from symptoms and cures from causes and to prescribe courses of action. Frames may be used to list symptoms, causes, cures, and the relationships between them.

Interpretation/Analysis

Interpretive/analytic systems are those in which a certain situation has occurred, and the expert system is charged with:

- discovering what has happened

- why it has happened

- how it should be responded to

Analytic and diagnostic systems often are quite similar in their approaches to problem solution and in the problems they are asked to solve. They differ in that analysis is usually performed well after an event has transpired and when a known problem exists that must be investigated. Diagnostic systems, on the other hand, generally are employed closer in time to the problem or before a problem is even known to exist—in order to detect trouble.

Examples of interpretive/analytic systems include the following applications:

- *telephony special line fault analysis.* interpreting error codes generated by an Emergency 911 or a toll-free 800 number system to catch line problems at their inchoate stages

- *airline reservation/billing system use analysis.* analyzing CPU utilization in a large and complex reservation-handling system in order to suggest ways of making use of excess capacity on certain hardware and reducing the load on any overworked machines in a network

- *collateralized mortgage obligation document analysis.* interpreting a document that stipulates the terms of a legal/financial agreement between parties involved in the selling and pooling of residential mortgages

Knowledge Representation and Inference

In analytic systems, which may be either forward or backward chaining, rules may be used to decide on the interpretation of data and to infer relationships between data. Frames may be used to store common recommendations for action or commonly encountered problems.

Configuration/Selection

Configurative systems assemble components—anything from pieces of computer hardware to fragments of legal text. The skill in a configuration system lies in its ability to put parts together with the smallest waste of time, space, and energy and to do so with the least amount of error.

The first step in doing configuration is often selection, the task of choosing components that can fit together or will work together.

Selective systems can be built on their own as well (such as those that recommend software products, bank services, or stocks to customers after surveying customer needs).

Configurative/selective systems may perform the following tasks:

- tell a user which components should be included in a configuration or select items to recommend to the user

- match those components against components in stock

- give directions for their assembly or assemble them (for example, build a document)

Examples of configurative systems include the following applications:

- *insurance document drafting.* assembling a legal document explaining group insurance coverage to employees, a contract created by selecting thousands of fragments of text and putting them together in the proper order

- *food processing equipment assemblage.* configuring a myriad of food processing machines to produce a particular product with the least amount of trial-and-error shifting of components after the configuration (which would result in wasted product and equipment downtime)

- *telecommunications switching system mapping.* translating customer telephony needs into a switching system (made up of thousands of individual parts) of the proper size and functionality needed to meet the customer's requirements.

Knowledge Representation and Inference

Selection is usually accomplished through a combination of constraint-based exclusion and internally derived scales. *Constraint-based exclusion* uses rules to filter the list of items being considered. The rules look at the items one at a time and either select or reject them, creating two lists: one of acceptable items and the other of discarded items (for example, products to be recommended to the customer and products not to be recommended).

Internal scaling uses rules to rank the items being considered. Each item is assigned a weight, depending on how well that item satisfies the requests of the user. What emerges is a ranked list of items: those at the top being highly recommended, those in the middle only slightly recommended, and those at the bottom not recommended.

Both selective and configurative systems are usually forward chaining, because so many data on the components have to be collected before a decision can be made on which components to choose and how to fit them together. It doesn't make sense to hypothesize one configuration, disprove its validity when new components are added, and then reconfigure the whole system over and over, as would happen in backward chaining. Configurative rules may be used to infer relationships between components (assembly instructions on how to fit the pieces together) or to select proper components necessary for a given configuration (which pieces require which other pieces). Frames may be used to represent the components to be assembled or their constraints.

Anomaly Detection/Monitoring/Prediction

Anomaly Detection/Monitoring

Anomalies are situations that do not conform to past known patterns. And anomaly detection systems search for breaches or changes in existing patterns that may signal a problem or an opportunity in the making. They are often used to monitor an on-going process in order to alert users when an unusual event has occurred. Such systems most often work in realtime, serving as a second pair of eyes for the experts or as an early warning system for users.

Prediction

Predictive expert systems utilize pattern recognition to compare and contrast recent situations or facts with past situations or facts, to determine the following information:

- any similarities or differences that may allow the system to infer what might happen next

- which precursors to a certain type of situation might be identified to make its prediction easier in the future

- which aspects of past situations may aid the user in anticipating future similar situations

Examples of monitoring, anomaly detection, and predictive systems include the following applications:

- *paper manufacturing process control.* keeping a watchful eye on the flow of slurry and the addition of dyes during the paper-making process

- *foreign currency trading.* catching, pointing out, and offering realtime recommendations on how to capitalize on significant changes in financial markets when traders themselves suffer a temporary lapse of attention to the market

- *telecomm network fault detection.* discovering the existence of cable problems that may hamper the transmission of voice or data over phone lines.

Knowledge Representation and Inference

Rules in monitoring, anomaly detection, and predictive systems are frequently used to compare patterns of behavior (for example, how a machine or a market is acting now compared to how it acted just before it last crashed); inductive systems may be used to discover those patterns of behavior. Frames may then be used to represent the patterns of behavior to be discovered or examined by the rules.

Design

Design systems, depending on their sophistication, may be used to carry out the following tasks:

- create a template, plan, or rough draft to be used in accomplishing a given task (the more common use of a design expert system)

- design and then perform or test the task itself, showing the results to the user

Examples of design systems include the following applications:

- *database design.* assisting inexperienced programmers in the production of database models that conform to in-house relational database conventions

- *manufacturing-line creation.* designing the lengths, turn angles, and speeds of a variable-speed conveyor belt on which automotive glass is carried through its phases of manufacture

- *code generation.* building functional FORTRAN source code from specifications entered by non-programmers in pseudocode or natural language

Design systems often are forward chaining because they require a good deal of data before they can begin to propose reasonable designs.

Rules in design systems often refer to the ways in which a task may or may not be performed, say, the syntactical requirements that must be adhered to when creating FORTRAN source code (for example, the IF command in most versions of FORTRAN must eventually be followed by a THEN and concluded with an ENDIF command). Frames may contain lists of the subcomponents that go into a completed system (for example, the program name, the subroutines and library files to be included, then the variable declarations, and so on).

Scheduling/Planning

Scheduling/planning systems are assigned the job of making a certain number of actions occur within a certain length of time and usually at a given cost. This temporal component, the preoccupation with time, separates scheduling systems from most other expert systems (although monitoring and predictive systems may also require an eye on the clock).

Examples of scheduling/planning systems include the following applications:

- *pharmaceutical laboratory work flow creation.* scheduling the use of and the facilities/supplies that will be required to use a series of specialized laboratories according to the schedules and needs of lab-using scientists and the requisite setup and breakdown times for equipment in the lab

- *shop-floor scheduling.* rescheduling the use of tooling machines after partial equipment failure, so that delays in production due to the breakdowns are minimized

- *tax form processing.* scheduling the passage of tax forms through the process of opening, sorting, numbering, prioritizing, correcting, keying in of data, and archiving

Knowledge Representation and Inference

Scheduling systems are usually forward chaining, collecting more or less complete information on the tasks to be scheduled before arranging them.

Scheduling rules may contain the following:

- the constraints under which goal states can be reached (for example, this scientist will not be in town on Wednesday, or this equipment cannot be removed from Lab 4 until 3 p.m.)

- the means of achieving goal states (for example, what has to be done to disassemble a machine and move it to another lab)

Frames may be used to represent the following:

- the features to be scheduled (the scientists, the room, the equipment)

- the goal states to be reached (such as having three particular chemists in a lab on Wednesday morning with the correct spectroscopy equipment installed and standing by)

- the desirable intermediary states (having the equipment in the lab by Tuesday night)

A Note on Paradigm Interpretation

Paradigms are flexible enough to allow a wide degree of interpretative license. What one KE classifies as, say, a diagnostic system, another may label as analytic or predictive.

For example, an expert system built to assist bond traders may be called any of the following:

- an anomaly detective system, because it offers warnings and signals buying opportunities by recognizing when ordinary technical analysis patterns (for example, "flags," "ascending top resistance levels," or "head-and-shoulders" patterns) have been broken

- an interpretive/analytic system, because it makes sense of great quantities of interacting data (for example, price, volume, open interest, trading activity, market movements)

- a diagnostic system, because it offers a solution to the problem of losing money on faulty trades

- a scheduling system, because it advises on the timing of trades

- a configuration system, because it configures a portfolio based on the constraints of minimal risk and maximal yield

An expert system's paradigm, therefore, is sometimes in the eye of the beholder.

Purposes

Just as there are certain general types of problem solution, there are
also general purposes to which expert systems are put.

Advisory Systems

The most common purpose for which expert systems are used is advice
giving. Advisory systems ordinarily are employed on a daily basis by a
user whose own skills are supplemented by the expert system. They
generally do not replace domain experts. Instead, they are used to
disseminate the unique knowledge of experienced individuals to a larger
audience. Such systems typically offer recommendations on a course of
action, as well as some explanation of the reasoning behind the recommendation, allowing the user to follow the system's suggestions or not.

Advisory system applications range from process control expert
systems for powdered milk processing to commodity options trad-
ing/timing systems. Help desks (hotlines) are a common type of advisory
system. They are typically built in the following circumstances:

- when interface with the public or another branch of an
  organization is required (by phone or directly)

- when the people who are giving advice at that interface are either
  scantily trained or highly trained but scarce

- when training more people or developing manuals does not seem
  to solve the problem of customers getting accurate, timely,
  correct-the-first-time information, or when the products/services
  on which the advice is given frequently increase in number or
  complexity

- when the problems encountered by the typical interface person
  are so various that no one person could easily master the entire
  range

- when advice/diagnosis must be given quickly to be of any use

Consultancy Systems

Consultancy expert systems often fulfill the same function as advisory
systems, but they are utilized only when something has gone wrong,
rather than on a daily basis. In fact, they often are built specifically
because serious problems occur so seldom in a field that people trained
to handle the problem have forgotten their training by the time the

situation occurs (such as in recovering from large computer system crashes). Consultancy systems, then, are used as much for their faultless memories as for their quick and intelligent response to problems.

Consultancy systems generally pay for themselves by operating in high-cost/high-risk areas in which there are few experts. They may, in fact, greatly reduce the need for experts in a given domain once they have proved effective. Consultancy systems often are narrowly focused *FDIR* (fault detection, isolation, and recovery) expert systems and are usually employed to rapidly diagnose the reasons for some kind of significant failure. They typically offer suggestions as to the causes of a problem, identify side effects (from the cause or from the suggested response) to watch out for, and recommend solutions.

Consultancy system applications range from jet engine failure diagnosis to automatic teller machine network fault detection to electrical failure FDIR systems in the suits of astronauts doing extra-vehicular work.

Tutorial Systems

Tutorial systems assist in the creation of new experts in a given field. They are generally utilized during the training of users rather than during actual operations. Tutorial systems justify their costs by ensuring that all trainees are exposed to situations necessary for their own future success in the domain (especially in dealing with customers).

Tutorial expert systems include "Socratic tutors," which present a case to the users and then critique the users on their solution of the case, and cognitive emulation systems, which ask the users to input a scenario to be solved by the system (which explains its reasoning as it solves the problem).

Tutorial applications range from pedagogic aids for property insurance underwriters to systems for the training of apprentice mechanics.

Proxy Systems

Proxy systems are the rarest of all expert system application types. They are designed to entirely supplant human domain experts. But because domain experts often will not cooperate in their own displacement, proxy systems are sometimes difficult to build for political, personnel, and job security reasons. As a result, most successful commercial proxy systems have been built not with the goal of eliminating experts, but with the aim of retaining "institutional memory."

Institutional (or "corporate") memory involves the preservation within an organization of experience and knowledge so valuable as to be worth capturing from retiring experts. The domain experts for such proxy systems are usually highly skilled long-time employees or company founders whose unique skills will be invaluable for decision making after the experts have retired. In such cases, experts are not only not hostile to the cloning of their expertise, but generally quite flattered. The expert system becomes, in a sense, their chance for immortality. And the opportunity to continue influencing a corporation after retirement is often powerful motivation for a company founder who has raised a business up from a pup.

Proxy applications built for corporate memory purposes range from expert systems for large-scale real estate development planning to those for scheduling petrochemical pipeline flows.

Front- and Back-End Systems

Expert systems usually are used in conjunction with conventional systems or with databases. In such an environment, front-end expert systems may act as filters that restrict or sift through data before they enter a database. And back-end systems typically serve as interpreters of data exiting a database. (Back-end systems are often inductive rather than deductive.) Front- and back-end expert system applications range from design-specification capture systems for complex engineering processes (in which the front-end expert system filters engineering spec data and places what it recognizes as relevant data into the correct database records or relations) to credit card fraud-detection inductive pattern discovery systems tied to a database of past known fraudulent transactions (in which the back-end expert system searches the database looking for new patterns that may be used in the future to recognize fraud).

Speculative Systems

Systems whose purpose is "speculation" (also called *what-if analysis*) are usually interpretive and diagnostic in nature. Such systems predict what would happen if a certain set of factors occurred together. Hypothetical data are typically offered to the expert system, and the system then gives warnings or recommendations for action in the event that the hypothetical circumstances occur.

Any expert system can be used for speculation, but those that are designed specifically for that purpose usually have well-developed and lucid user interfaces (which are sometimes adapted for people more comfortable with, say, spreadsheet analysis or CAD/CAM graphical representation of data).

Knowledge Acquisition 6

The Knowledge Engineer as Cognitive Psychologist

Knowledge acquisition is the process of interviewing an expert in a particular domain and then translating the knowledge gleaned in those interviews into machine readable code. But there is more to knowledge acquisition than simple stenography. Knowledge acquisition requires that the KE actually *understand* the domain the system is being built in, as well as the motivations and needs of the people cooperating in the project.

With this in mind, a KE should approach the knowledge acquisition sessions in three phases: before, during, and after the interviews. Each phase has its important elements.

Before the Interviews

Understanding the Expert's Motivation

Some understanding of the expert's incentive in cooperating in the system's development will be invaluable when future problems inevitably arise. The worst experts are those who cooperate reluctantly:

- the experts who cooperate because they feel threatened in some way

- the experts whose high-status jobs will disappear when the system is built

70

- the experts whose rare (and personally profitable) skills will become commonly available once the system is built

In most of these cases, an expert system should not even be attempted, because it will prove impossible to build a system against the will of the expert.

The best experts, on the other hand, are those who have some private motive for seeing the system successfully implemented:

- the retiring expert who founded the company and who wants his or her expertise to continue to nurture the corporate child

- the expert who is doing an onerous but important job and has been promised more interesting work if the system succeeds

- the expert who takes pride in being selected for the task and who knows his or her name will be associated with the project when it succeeds

Knowing why an expert is cooperating in the system's construction will help in resolving political problems that rear up late in a system's development. And just knowing that an expert sincerely backs the system's completion can go a long way toward saving a threatened project (see Chapter 10 "Common Problems"). Such support can also accelerate the development of a project because it provides the impetus to plow through technical difficulties.

Understanding the Organization's Motivation

The best reasons for an organization to pursue an expert system application include the following:

- supplementing the skills of experts who occasionally suffer costly lapses of attention (for example, foreign exchange traders)

- distributing expertise evenly throughout a group (for example, to help desk personnel)

- increasing the speed, accuracy, or throughput of current operations (for example, the configuration of complex computer hardware)

- keeping the hiring of new employees down by increasing the productivity of current employees (for example, the scheduling of jet engine maintenance)

- training new experts (for example, property/casuality insurance underwriting)

- creating new expertise (for example, inductive case-based systems)

  The worst reasons for building an expert system include:

- Trying to circumvent an organization's political problems by building an expert system around them. An example would be when workers in one plant do not have access to experts in another plant because of squabbling managers or arguments over turf. The way to resolve such a political problem—when people in different plants cannot talk to each other—is political in nature: replacing managers, pairing specific workers with specific experts, opening up the lines of communication, or at the very least, having the two groups exchange phone numbers. An expert system that clones the experts in one plant for the workers in the other plant is just a palliative, not a solution. And it is not worth the expense and time involved to build an expert system to get around such an obviously political problem.

- Tricking experts into replacing themselves (or their co-workers) with an expert system. An example would be building an expert system to replace systems analysts in a large COBOL DP shop. Promising one analyst that he will retain his job if he helps build the expert system is the same as asking the analyst to put his friends out of work. Such a situation will become a powderkeg just waiting for stray sparks to ignite it. Even if the expert cooperates, his own dismissal will certainly be in his mind when he knows he's dealing with such a devious organization.

- Building an expert system for public relations purposes. An example would be building an expert system because everyone else in the industry seems to have one or because the board of directors wants to talk about the company's state-of-the-art AI work at the next stockholders' meeting. An organization motivated to produce AI window dressing may not want to wrangle with the tough technical, organizational, and financial details that will arise as the system evolves. People working in such a political climate may have only one eye on the expert system; the other eye will be on robotics or neural nets or whatever else seems glamorous enough to become the focus of the company's next hi-tech PR campaign.

Domain experts are usually time-pressured individuals. KEs know that *the expert they* most *want to talk to is the one the company can* least *afford to spare* for interviews. As a result, an organization takes pains to shield its experts from outside demands on their time. And, since knowledge acquisition interviews constitute a demand on the expert's time, they have to be kept concise and productive. This means that the KE should expend a good deal of initial effort reviewing information that is already available *before* beginning to interview the expert and codifying the expert's specific reasoning processes.

If existing written material in a given domain appears valid (for example, recent books or manuals, especially those written by the expert), the KE should begin by digesting that material and reforming it into knowledge representation schemes. If there are reports on successfully solved past problems, it may be possible to build a small prototype based entirely on those reports to show the expert at the *first* interview.

If report or textbook information is non-existent, invalid, or obviously antiquated, it may be possible to interview expert-support people first (assistants, backups) to establish a groundwork and gather enough information to bring an embryonic prototype to an early meeting with a harried expert.

What results from this kind of serious homework on the part of the KE—whatever the merits of the first prototype—are a clearer impression of the task the expert performs, an understanding of the elementary rules that will be used by the expert, and some acquaintance with the unique vocabulary of the domain. And the expert may more readily accept a KE who is willing to put in time learning about the field, especially when the expert can see palpable results on the computer screen early in the process.

Coding

It is always easier for an expert to look at a prototype and answer the question "Is this how you do it?" than it is to respond to "How do you perform your decision making?"

So, an ambitious KE's goal is to walk into the first or second interview with a prototype ready to show to the expert. This is possible because many expert performances are the result of *both* book learning *and* empirical domain experience. And the knowledge derived from books, manuals, and reports can be encoded into an expert system's foundation even before the KE has a firm grasp of the expert's unique methods of operation.

During the Interviews

Establishing a Schedule

The first few interviews with an expert will, necessarily, be impromptu affairs. But once the prototype is underway, it is generally easier for everyone to abide by a set schedule. And regular interviews can be arranged so they inconvenience the expert as little as possible.

It is always best *not* to interview an expert, then do something else for a month, eventually getting back to the expert weeks later. Schedules should be adjusted so the KE can dedicate time to the prototype immediately after the first interviews and strike while the iron is hot.

When the expert is in close physical proximity to the KE, one or two hours a week is a common interview arrangement. If the expert is some distance away (perhaps in another state), the interview schedule may be devised on a monthly basis, calling for several days of long intensive interviews followed by three weeks of coding with occasional phone calls in between. In fact, this latter scenario is often the most productive arrangement because when the KE travels a great distance to attend the interview, both the KE and the expert tend to be prepared, focused, and dedicated to the task of building the expert system.

To save the expert time, some interviews can be conducted over lunch. Or meetings can be set up for the longest reasonable time, say two hours, and any extra minutes that appear at the end of the interview can be given back to the grateful expert as free time. (This is better than arranging a short meeting and running overtime.)

Friday afternoons at 4 p.m. often are the ideal time for efficient interviews because everyone is usually motivated to contribute lucid responses, solve problems, and then get home. This approach doesn't apply when workaholics are involved, but in most cases it helps to force concision and brevity. Conducting the interview in an office in which there are no chairs also works.

Focusing on the Highest Payoff

When trying to narrow down the problem space to an area that can be treated by the first prototype (called *scoping* the problem), the KE should choose the area that promises the highest return on invested time and energy. Ask the expert, manager, or users, "Where does it hurt the most? What would you most like to see this expert system accomplish?" Wherever the pain level is highest is the place to begin coding the prototype.

For example, if the application involves creating an expert system to advise users who answer customer questions at a telecomm equipment telephone help desk, and two-thirds of all requests are for information on communications problems, communications, then, is the area in which to begin coding. It may be tempting to begin coding with hardware problems—which may constitute only 3% of all customer requests—just to feel a sense of closure when that small part of the expert system is done. But building the hardware part of the knowledgebase may require just as much time as building a communications segment, even though its payoff (that is, its usefulness) to the organization would be far smaller.

The Three Phases of an Interview

A knowledge acquisition interview can be divided chronologically into three segments: old business, present business, and future business.

Old business, the first topic discussed in an interview, has to do with anything the KE has failed to understand or has been unable to implement since the last interview. It may include misunderstandings of domain vocabulary or of the expert's approach to problem solution. An example of an old business question is, "I don't think I quite understand when you would purchase a collateralized mortgage obligation. Could you talk about that one again?"

Present business involves a look at the latest prototype, followed by discussion of how and where it should be expanded and improved. This is usually the heart of the interview, the part that takes the most time. An example of a present business question is, "The system now treats CMOs as just another security, as you can see here on the screen. Is that a fair assumption on the system's part, or should there really be a separate category for CMOs?"

Future business, which usually concludes an interview, involves discussion of anticipated problems or possible changes in the system's problem-solving approach when new features are incorporated into the system. An example of a future business discussion is, "The system now thinks of zero coupon bonds as securities that generate no interest but that appreciate in value. The IRS, however, sees a year's appreciation in value as equivalent to a year's interest accrual, even though the bond holder doesn't actually receive the money until redemption. That means we're being taxed on money we won't receive for several years. We'll

---

be adding this kind of tax knowledge to the expert system soon, so how the system handles zero coupon bonds in the future may have to change. For purposes of this expert system, should we treat them as interest bearing or not?"

Using Real Cases

When testing the expert system in front of the expert, the KE should choose typical cases and review how the system and the expert solve them. Rather than inventing hypothetical scenarios, select actual past cases, the more recent the better. This will give the system some measure of immediacy and ground it in the real world. Invented cases too often are sanitized or purified. Real life is messy. And the solution of real cases does more to gain the expert's confidence in the system than any purified solutions could.

If the expert says, "There are no typical cases. All cases are different," then choose one at random to begin with. If the cases are, in fact, all different, it doesn't matter which one is chosen. If the cases are not all different, that fact will gradually become apparent in future sessions.

Don't ignore exceptions, special cases, or unique situations. But don't dwell on them in the beginning. Concentrate on solving typical cases first. They will point to the representation schemes to consider and the inference mechanisms to think about. Exceptions (which can be handled by rule daemons, additional object attributes, additional rule premises, or an exception slot in a frame) can be built in as the system matures.

Pursuing Both Depth and Breadth

Expert systems usually ask a user both general and detailed questions. The general questions help the system identify a particular area to focus on. The detailed questions explore that area in depth. This is especially true of diagnostic systems.

For example, a diagnostic system to identify and repair malfunctions in electronic equipment will ask several questions just to classify the problem type or to locate where in the equipment the malfunction has occurred. Once it has done that, the system will ask specific questions to correct that particular malfunction. The general questions provide breadth to the system; the specific questions depth.

A KE has to find out in an interview both the number of things that the expert does (breadth) and how much the expert knows about certain things (depth). Only then can the KE build an initial prototype that encompasses some depth and some breadth. This means that during an interview the KE has to ask the expert questions to reveal how many topics the expert system should handle and how carefully it should treat them.

For example, a question for the expert that would bring out the system's breadth is, "What are all the possible things that could go wrong with the equipment?" The answer to this question will suggest how broad the expert system must be to be useful.

A question that would suggest where the system's depth should then be concentrated is, "Which pieces of equipment fail most often?" The answer to this question will tell the KE where to begin fleshing out the knowledgebase. And a question that would begin to handle that depth is, "When X malfunctions in this particular way, what do you do to correct it?" The expert's answer to this question will add detailed knowledge to the system.

Questions to Ask

There are no magical incantations in knowledge acquisition. KE's just keep their goal in mind (creation of a *useful* expert system) and ask everything necessary to accomplish that goal. But there are some commonly asked questions:

Describe your job.
(The answer will separate the task into its numeric and heuristic parts.)

Could we do a typical case?

What are your most common problems?

Is a training manual available?

How were you trained?
(The answer will help the KE estimate how long it might take to build the expert system.)

How do you know to do that at this particular time?
(The answer will indicate rule interactions.)

What information do you use when you make that decision?
(The answer will indicate frame components.)

How much time do you spend at this task?
(The answer will indicate time savings and return on investment [ROI].)

What would you do if you didn't have to do this job?
(The system shouldn't clone someone's only job or the only job from
which they gain status in the organization.)

What are the most important parts of your job?
(The answer will indicate the parts to encode first into the expert
system.)

Where did you get that information from?
(The answer will indicate cues and props used by the expert.)

*What category does this fall under? How many parts does this have?
What is the relationship between this part and that one?*
(The answer will indicate inheritance hierarchies.)

*Does the time at which this occurs matter? Does it have to happen
before that?*
(The answer will indicate temporal constraints, especially in
scheduling and process control systems.)

*Does that happen if either of these things occurs, or if both of them
occur?*
(The answer will clarify rule premises.)

What pieces of information are needed to make that decision?
(The answer will fill in the left-hand side of a rule, the premises.)

What would be the possible results of that occurring?
(The answer will fill in the right-hand side of a rule, the conclusions.)

Why would you recommend this solution for the problem?
(The answer will offer explanations.)

How sure are you that that situation will result from these factors?
(The answer will indicate certainty factors.)

*Does this problem also tell you you should look at that? When this
level rises, does that one also rise by the same amount? When this
happens, do you know it will always lead to that?*
(The answer will indicate associations, correlations, and transitivity.)

*What is X like? Could the problem be something other than X? If X
happens, should Y always or never happen too?*
(The answer will indicate analogies, substitutions, and constraints.)

Can you give me an example of X?
(The answer will indicate objects in a class.)

What general category do you think X would be an example of?
(The answer will indicate a class into which to put an object.)

Compiling a Domain Lexicon

An attentive KE will write down domain jargon and technical terms as they crop up and create a glossary that grows as the system grows. It can be used to refresh the memory of a KE who is building several subsystems simultaneously. And it will drastically reduce the learning curve for all who follow the first KE into a new domain.

Suitable definitions in a glossary include the following items:

- professional slang (*example*: "They tried using a tin parachute as an LBO shark repellent. But when the porcupine provision didn't work, they looked for a white knight." *translation*: "The company tried to stave off a leveraged buyout by legally guaranteeing huge severance bonuses to all employees discharged by any new owner. But because a legal loophole was found in that arrangement, the target company had to seek out a friendly buyer who would be more likely to leave the company intact after purchasing it.")

- domain jargon (*example*: "wire house"; *translation*: "large brokerage house")

- technical terms (*example*: "positive yield curve"; *translation*: "when long-term debt security rates are higher than short-term rates")

- terms invented by the expert (*example*: "bellyflop"; *translation*: "rapid fall of a newly issued stock")

The Telephone Test

If an expert uses a lot of cues in the performance of his job, it may be difficult to separate the cues from the knowledge. For example, an expert who listens to the hum of machinery and recognizes impending trouble by the pitch of the motors may have difficulty answering the question, "How did you know the machine was about to break down?" His response may be, "I just knew. That's all."

To separate the expert from his or her cues, the KE's traditional technique has always been the telephone test. The expert is installed in a room away from cues. The KE calls the expert on the phone and presents a problem. The expert then solves the problem by telling the KE to look in a particular manual, or to listen for the grinding of gears, or to see whether the X coordinate is above 100 on a certain graph. Because the expert cannot connect with any of the cues, or ponies, he or she must do what the expert system will eventually do—tell the user how to find the necessary information and what to do with it when it has been found.

If this method seems too affected or cumbersome, the KE can sit in the room with the expert, with all necessary manuals on only the KE's side of the table. The expert is then required to describe the correct cues, and the proper manual to read, but is not allowed to touch them. In this way, the expert's cues and props are made useful to an untrained user.

Rules

Don't force the expert to become a KE.

Insulate the expert from daily coding concerns. If the expert wants to see some code, show the easiest or most representative samples. A KE's first job is to learn from the expert, not to teach the expert.

Think as the expert thinks.

Knowledge engineering is similar to method acting in that KEs, in a sense, become the characters they portray. They read what the experts read. They begin to use jargon appropriately. In time, they get as excited as the experts when they see an inverted yield curve, or a telecomm network glitch, or a new custom-made VLSI chip design. They absorb not only the expert's knowledge, but also the concern for the job. And that concern eventually shows up in the expert system's performance.

Listen.

Nodding, smiling, and saying to the expert, "I see, I see," accomplishes nothing if the knowledge engineer is actually sitting in the office chair having an out-of-body experience. Lying on a black sand beach in Aruba, listening to the rustle of palm trees overhead and the splash of flamingoes in a distant saltpond is something to do *after* the knowledge acquisition sessions. Time is just too short during a session.

The longest knowledge acquisition sessions are usually at the beginning of a project, when everyone is most enthusiastic. But even then, they cannot be time-wasting affairs for the expert. It is important that the sessions be productive. And that requires serious listening on the KE's part.

The user of the expert system is always right.

Building an expert system in accordance with the user's needs is one way to make sure the system actually will be used when it is fielded.

The users may not understand the representation schemes involved, the interface contraints, the main memory limitations, or the programmer's desire for elegant coding. But they know what they want and what the expert system should do for them. So the users should be the ultimate arbiters of the system's final functionality and features.

Bring a tape recorder (and let the expert know about it).

One of the great disasters of knowledge acquisition is to spend three days with an expert, scribbling mountains of notes, only to return to the office and not understand what on earth the notes mean. At the time of the meeting, they may have looked perfectly lucid. But after a few days, when looked at out of context, they revert to inscrutable scribble. And the KE ends up calling the expert a dozen times to clarify his own notes.

Using a tape recorder can help prevent this problem. But it should not be used without the expert's permission. The expert's trust is mandatory, and sneaking a tape recorder into a session may spell doom for the expert system when the subterfuge is revealed. If the expert is agreeable, tape recording is one way to ensure that knowledge acquisition sessions are productive and won't have to be repeated. The tapes also allow KEs just joining a project to catch up on interviews without having to bother the expert with elementary questions again.

Some experts will object to a tape recorder because the tapes might be given to their bosses, or because they dislike the sound of their voices on tape, or because they're afraid they may sound disorganized. Giving the tapes back to the expert after coding may assuage these fears, as may promising that no one else will listen to the tapes.

Repeat concepts back to the expert.

The best way to learn something is to teach it. A KE who tries, in a sense, to teach back to the expert what the KE has just learned will have to formulate his or her thoughts clearly. This clarification will be useful later on when the knowledge is being encoded. Also, the expert will be able to discern whether the KE actually understands the task.

After the Interviews

Breaking Down the Problem

Any large expert system is divisible into several parts. Some of those parts are more important than others. And some parts are necessary only when the expert system approaches completion. After one or two interviews, the various segments of a knowledgebase will become apparent. It is then that the KE can begin to divide programming tasks into manageable pieces, focusing on the parts that are more important and leaving the rest for later.

Writing Short Reports

To keep everyone on the project team apprised of the system's progress, the KE should write occasional reports detailing what has been accomplished so far. The reports serve as a record of the project's growth and inform the various participants about the system to which they are all contributing. They convey the impression that the system is moving forward, not stagnating. Reports also are reassuring to people new to expert system development, people who may not be confident about the system's final outcome. Funders and managers who may have no understanding of technical issues will understand a report's "works now" or "doesn't work yet." The reports sometimes even clarify issues for the KE. And they serve as valuable reading material for project members who join the project in progress.

Pages from a Knowledge Engineer's Notebook:
A KE's Report on Domain Information Gathered Before the First Expert Interview

Preliminary Knowledge Acquisition Report

    Domain: Hydrocarbon exploration

    Project task: Sedimentology/stratigraphy

    Paradigm: Diagnosis/configuration

    Purpose: Advisory/proxy

    CC: manager, project funder, other KEs, domain expert, database manager

The Domain

Stratigraphic analysis of drill core samples involves the study of cylinders of rock pulled from the earth's crust. Its goal is to identify the various layers of rock beneath the surface, layers that were created as sediment sank to the bottom of a body of water and was buried and compressed.

Analyzing and making sense of these various patterns of layered sediment will be the purpose of the expert system.

The Task

The task begins when a drill is sent down to pull up a tube (core) of rock. When the core sample is pulled from its bore hole and sent to the lab, the characteristics of each layer of sediment in the sample are noted. The layers are grouped together, and the groupings are studied for features or contiguities that suggest the presence of oil-bearing formations.

How Knowledge Is Represented

Stratigraphic analysts first look at layers of deposit called facies. Facies often occur together in recognizable sequences called parasequences. Several contiguous parasequences may form a parasequence set. And several sets together may constitute an identifiable pattern known as a depositional system. Any of these patterns—systems, sets, parasequences—may indicate the presence of oil beneath the surface.

The clearly hierarchical form that the knowledge takes suggests object- or frame-based representation (packages of facts). Each facies becomes a frame full of data on the thickness of the deposit, the type of rock within it, and its distinguishing characteristics (such as holes made by ancient burrowing animals). Parasequences, sets, and depositional systems (all supersets of facies) look like higher-order frames (general classes) into which the smaller frames (specific layers) fit. Conclusions about the presence of oil-bearing formations can be drawn from each frame (the facies) and from their contiguity (in parasequences, sets, and depositional systems).

An Example

For instance, a facies of coarse calcareous clay chips suggests an ancient sea beach (the calcium in the clay being from limestone, from the shells of mollusks). A facies above that one (deposited later), consisting of

---

fine-grained silt, suggests the effluent of a river emptying into the ocean (bringing soil washed down from the highlands). A silty shale facies deposited on top of the previous layers and still showing the ripples of ocean currents suggests the expansion of the river into the sea. Together these three facies constitute a pattern: the formation, over millenia, of an ancient river delta, a promising site for further hydrocarbon exploration.

The Expert System

The expert's role in this sort of stratigraphic analysis is to use every scrap of information contained in sedimentology books and picked up through experience to recognize patterns that suggest the presence of hydrocarbons. In this particular case, we will be able to bring a foundation prototype to the first acquisition session with the expert just by reading appropriate texts.

Pages from a Knowledge Engineer's Notebook:
Transcription of Notes Taken During an Early Knowledge Acquisition Session

> Domain: Corrugatorboard manufacturing
>
> Project task: Scheduling of material shipments
>
> Paradigm: Forecasting/planning/scheduling
>
> Purpose: Advisory/proxy
>
> CC: manager, project funder, other KEs, domain expert, database manager

Background

Corrugatorboard is the material used to make packing boxes. Usually, it is made of three layers of paper joined together. The outer two layers (liner) of double-faced corrugatorboard are smooth and flat. The middle layer (the medium) is corrugated to provide strength to the finished box.

The rolls of paper that go into creating corrugatorboard are roughly 10 feet in height and 6 feet in diameter. Their storage requires a good deal of space. And a plant that runs out of rollstock cannot make corrugatorboard, but a plant cannot store more than a four-week supply of any one type of stock.

Shipments are made every three weeks by rail car from the paper manufacturing plant, but the cars are limited in their capacity. And several different types of paper are used in corrugatorboard manufacture, not all of which need to be in stock all the time. So, forecasting which types of paper will be needed when and scheduling the corrugator to make the right types of boxes for on-time delivery are crucial tasks. Only one plant in the country has a scheduler/forecaster who consistently does optimal scheduling. He never runs out of stock or misses a promised delivery date for boxes—he is the expert we want to clone.

The Forecasting Expert System

The task of forecasting (predicting anticipated rollstock needs) calls for the following skills on the part of the expert:

- Pattern recognition—recognizing the effects of past ordering decisions, understanding historical box sales patterns, matching available paper supplies to available corrugator board plants, and knowing the grade/width needs of different box types.

- Non-monotonicity—the ability to handle new or changed schedules on the fly.

- Hybrid thinking—deciding which formulas to apply and when. A hybrid expert system combines AI and formulaic programming. The intelligence in such a system is the same type of intelligence used by the human expert, whose gift is for selecting the appropriate materials planning formula for a given situation, not just typing numbers into a calculator.

Definitions

Forecasting

The task of ordering rollstock (liner and medium) from mills and seeing to inventory replenishment. A just-in-time (JIT) balancing act: trying to keep inventory low without running out of liner or medium paper. This is usually done once a fortnight or once a month (ideally should probably be done once a week).

Scheduling

The task of scheduling jobs on the corrugator (the equipment that makes the boxes). This type of scheduling is usually done once every three days. It may have to be redone at short notice because of sudden changes: equipment breakdown, rush orders coming in, sudden shifts in priorities, or insufficient rollstock in inventory.

Final Numbers

The calculated numbers that give the expert an idea of how much of each rollstock will have to be ordered to keep up with demand. "Final" is deceptive, however, because the "final number" by itself is of little use. It has to be "massaged" considerably before it can be used to predict rollstock needs. It does not consider deductions for rollstock in inventory, backordered or in-transit stock, historical usage, grade/width considerations, or forecasted box sales. Adjusting the raw final number to a sensible one is where the forecaster's expertise resides.

Conclusions of Knowledge Acquisition Meeting

Expert System's Purpose

"Master scheduling" of the entire flow of materials from the incoming paper to the outgoing boxes. Handling of changes in orders and flow maintenance.

Stated Objectives

Quality/productivity enhancement, improved service, increased throughput, operating expense reduction, inventory control.

Unstated Goals

JIT or JALL (just a little late) system, flow control, inventory reduction, market share increase, freight cost reduction, increased profitability, greater forecasting abilities, better scheduling/planning.

Current Problems

Balancing of liner and medium is a crucial problem at the moment, involving the following factors:

1. Matching various grades coming in. Some grades of medium can be used only with certain grades of liner, so the equation may not be as simple as two liners for one medium. Some types of box use two (triple-faced) mediums or three (quadruple-faced) mediums, which confounds the problem of scheduling/prediction of inventory.

2. Correlating all the disparate parts of the ordering/forecasting process.

3. The ability to cope with on-the-fly changes in the schedule.

4. Grade/width usage forecasting.

Potentially Troublesome Areas: Factors Beyond Our Control

It is difficult to control outside mills that produce paper rollstock. They will always be a wild card in the forecasting/scheduling task because we cannot anticipate their breakdowns.

Also, sales people often don't get their orders in on time. Sometimes they make promises without checking first on stock availability and schedules, and may set unrealistic deadlines for the plant to meet.

Possible Arguments Against Construction of the Forecasting Expert System

Q **Is availability of *information* the real problem in forecasting, not the lack of forecasting *expertise*? Does the expert actually possess some unique information not available to other plant forecasters, or is he just better at utilizing information available to everyone?**

A *The domain expert does not seem to possess any information that would be unavailable to other plant forecasters/schedulers. Part of his expertise appears to be in making greater use of the information he has (information that everyone else also has access to).*

Q **Is there true expertise involved or just sophisticated number crunching?**

A *The final number is spit out at the end of a formula. Creation of this number is already automated. But the figure is of relatively little value. Plant stock forecasters who use only this figure seldom balance their shipments adequately. The figure must be considerably "adjusted" by the forecaster before it is usable. This is where the expertise (expert system) lies.*

Current Knowledge Acquisition Focus

We are focusing on the rollstock forecasting task first, since that seems to be the greater need and will give the higher return on our invested time. We are defining, with the expert, the factors that go into reshaping the final figure, because skill at reshaping the figure is what sets this particular expert apart from other plant schedulers. We are defining the influence of various factors on the final number, among them:

- the amount of rollstock in inventory
- backordered stock about to be shipped
- in-transit stock about to be delivered
- historical usage patterns for different box types
- grade/width considerations
- forecasted box sales according to season

The components with the greatest heuristic content are historical pattern recognition and box sale forecasting.

We currently are building an inductive system to recognize patterns of historical usage. This system uses data from the purchase database in which all box orders for the past nineteen years have been stored. We are looking for patterns of purchase according to the following factors:

- season (boxes for strawberries in the early summer, apples in the fall)
- box type (bleached white outer liner or ordinary brown unbleached)
- box dimensions
- number of medium strips (strength and rigidity considerations)
- the salesperson involved

The expert has been particularly helpful in suggesting these criteria as the ones most likely to yield useful patterns. When this system is completed, we will have induced a collection of heuristics useful for forecasting box sales and future rollstock needs on a week-to-week basis.

Knowledge Representation 7

The Knowledge Engineer as Epistemologist

Knowledge representation is simply a way of organizing knowledge inside an expert system. Representation refers to the packaging, storage, and manipulation of knowledge in an expert system by methods called *schemes.* Just as the "record" and the "relation" are the schemes used in databases to package data, the "frame," the "rule," and their variations are the formats used in expert systems to bundle knowledge.

Selecting the appropriate knowledge representation schemes to use in a given application is the first step in coding an expert system. The representation choices made at the start of a project will influence tool selection, program performance, and the functionality of the system later on. But choosing knowledge representation schemes need first not be a gruelingly painful process. In many cases, the schemes will simply fall out at the start of the project. Certain schemes will appear obvious when the application and the users' needs are understood.

In this chapter, cases are presented first not because they are the most common representation schemes (they are not), but because the creation of knowledge in any domain generally proceeds from the recognition of individual cases to the recognition of general rules and principles. So in the following section, we'll look at inductive schemes (dealing with individual cases) before going on to deductive schemes (dealing with general principles).

Cases

When no expert exists for a given task, but a great deal of data is available, the knowledge representation scheme often employed is the *case*. The choice of this particular representation is, in a sense, already made by the constraints inherent in such a project. The absence of a domain expert means there will be no rules available to the KE. And the existence of copious data means there will be past examples for the expert system to study.

Cases are essentially frames (blocks of data) that contain factual "snapshots" of a situation. They often reveal what occurred during a particular event and what preceded or followed that event. The implied connection is that the first event caused or led to the succeeding event. So by studying many past cases, the expert system can understand cause-and-effect relationships in past events and use that understanding to solve problems in cases it has never seen before.

For instance, a particular case-based configuration system has to solve the problem of creating quiet mufflers while maintaining automobile performance, a problem called muffler sonic resonance reduction. It does this by analyzing past muffler designs, noting their noise output, and then extrapolating new designs. In a sense, the system creates heuristics and formulas from raw data.

A muffler's purpose is to minimize engine noise. A muffler system comprises an exhaust manifold, which emerges from the engine, a catalytic converter, an initial pipe, a premuffler, a midpipe, a postmuffler, and a tailpipe. Manipulation of the muffler system's specifications (pipe girth, pipe length, and the area of resonance chambers inside the mufflers) allows engineers to design a car that meets noise pollution standards in various parts of the world, but still maintains high performance.

In this type of configuration application, cases are examples of old muffler systems. Every case in the system's casebase has two parts: a description of a past muffler system design and a description of the sonic effects of that design (how much noise is allowed to escape). For example,

Past Muffler System Design

Length of exhaust manifold: 22 cm

Diameter of exhaust manifold: 6 cm

Length of initial pipe: 22 cm

Diameter of initial pipe: 6 cm

Length of midpipe: 22 cm

Diameter of midpipe: 6 cm

Length of tailpipe: 22 cm

Diameter of tailpipe: 6 cm

Capacity of catalyzer resonance chamber: 134 ccm

Capacity of premuffler resonance chamber: 166 ccm

Capacity of postmuffler resonance chamber: 192 ccm

Sonic Effects of Past Muffler System Design

Sonic resonance volume (i.e., noise) at 35 Hz frequency : 2 dB

Sonic resonance volume at 80 Hz frequency : 26 dB

Sonic resonance volume at 200 Hz frequency : 35 dB

Sonic resonance volume at 500 Hz frequency : 47 dB

In this case, the inductive expert system does several things. First, it looks at a new case offered by its user. Then it compares that new case (new muffler design specifications) to the batch of other cases it knows about (the *training set*). It classifies the new case according to its understanding of the problem, that is, it finds the past cases most similar to the new case being investigated. Finally, it extrapolates anticipated noise volumes at particular frequencies from the old cases to the new one.

For example, the user gives the system the first half of a new case:

Length of exhaust manifold: 20 cm

Diameter of exhaust manifold: 5 cm

Length of initial pipe: 18 cm

Diameter of initial pipe: 4 cm

Length of midpipe: 15 cm

Diameter of midpipe: 6 cm

Length of tailpipe: 30 cm

Diameter of tailpipe: 6 cm

Capacity of catalyzer resonance chamber: 110 ccm

Capacity of premuffler resonance chamber: 97 ccm

Capacity of postmuffler resonance chamber: 204 ccm

The user then expects the system to return the second half of this case, based on a comparison with all the other cases it knows about:

Volume at 35 Hz frequency : 0 dB

Volume at 80 Hz frequency : 28 dB

Volume at 200 Hz frequency : 27 dB

Volume at 500 Hz frequency : 56 dB

The user is telling the system, "Here is a new muffler system I have built. Please tell me how much noise it will create." The user can also tell the system, "I have these resonance constraints to meet (noise volumes at different frequencies). Please give me the dimensions (lengths and diameters) of a muffler system that will meet them." In this second instance, the user presents the bottom half of a case and requires the system to produce the top half.

The KE's role in building a case-based expert system is twofold; both facets involve knowledge representation. The KE decides or discovers which characteristics of muffler design affect sonic resonance. Those important characteristics go into all cases in the form of *attributes*. For example, "length of tailpipe" is an attribute that has an obvious effect on engine noise, so it is a factor that will be looked at in each case. But "radiator size" has no effect on noise levels, so it is not included in any cases.

Deciding which attributes to put into a case is the single most critical aspect of building inductive expert systems, because an inductive system can infer only from the attributes that it knows about. If attributes are missing from the cases, the system is essentially blind to them. No inferencing can be done from missing attributes.

When the attributes to be installed in every case have been chosen (sometimes by trial and error to see which attributes affect the results, sometimes by interviewing people who are familiar with the domain, sometimes by statistical cluster analysis), the KE then has to determine how to define similarity between the new case and the old cases in the casebase. The expert system must be able to determine which cases are most similar to the new case under study. But "similar" may mean similar in effect on sonic resonance at 35 Hertz or at 80 Hertz, in total length of piping, or in any number of factors. So deciding which attributes will be most important in determining a new case's similarity with other cases has to be done early in a system's development.

For example, consider these two cases in a casebase:

Case 1

Attribute X: Yes

Attribute Y: Yes

Attribute Z: No

Attribute Q: Yes

Case 2

Attribute X: Yes

Attribute Y: No

Attribute Z: Yes

Attribute Q: No

Now say the following new case is presented to the system:

New Case

Attribute X: Yes

Attribute Y: Yes

Attribute Z: Yes

Which of the two cases in the casebase would the expert system choose as most similar to the new case? Both case 1 and case 2 differ from the new case by one value, so the answer will depend on whether attribute Y or attribute Z is judged to be more important in assessing similarity between cases. If attribute Y is given greater weight, the answer from the expert system will be "New Case: Attribute Q: Yes" because case 1 will be more similar to the new case than case 2. If attribute Z is more important, then "New Case: Attribute Q: No" will be the answer.

Determining which attributes are most important in predicting results is often done by iterative dichotomization, also known as ID3. ID3 involves taking statistical measures of the effects of certain attributes on final results (that is, it measures the effect of premise attributes on conclusion attributes). The method then looks at the number of cases and the frequency with which certain premise attributes correspond with certain conclusion attributes. The outcome is a determination of which attributes have the greatest influence on the results.

In many applications, this is as far as the expert system has to go. The user asks the system to analyze a new case in light of past situations and to make predictions based on those precedents. But in some applications, the expert system's purpose is not only to predict but to explain how predictions were arrived at. In fact, the system's purpose may not be to extrapolate from past cases at all but to induce rules from past cases.

In these situations (when the expert system is asked to explain its extrapolations or to create rules where none existed before), the system can focus on either the premise attributes or the conclusion attributes. When presented with these three cases, for example,

Attribute X: Yes	Attribute X: Yes	Attribute X: No
Attribute Y: No	Attribute Y: Yes	Attribute Y: No
Attribute Z: 5	Attribute Z: 5	Attribute Z: 7

and asked, "What effect does the premise Attribute X have?" the system will induce (in this case, by simple matching) the rule

IF attribute X = Yes
THEN attribute Z = 5

In fact, because the number of past cases here is so small, the system could also conclude

IF attribute X = No
THEN attribute Z = 7

This example involves inducing a rule from a case's premise attribute, but the system could just as well be asked to induce rules from conclusion attributes. For instance, the system could be asked to answer the question, "What factors would cause attribute Z to be 5?" The answer the system would offer would be

IF attribute Z = 5
THEN attribute X = Yes
AND attribute Y = NO with a probability of 1/2

In this way, an inductive system can devise rules by discovering patterns in past cases. It can create the knowledgebase for a deductive expert system by analyzing cases. In fact, it can build expertise in a domain in which there is currently no expertise. But to do any of these things effectively, a case-based system must have a large number of cases available for study. The more cases, the more accurate the inductive system's predictions and decisions will be and the more value the expert system will have to the organization.

Without a good many cases, a precedent-based expert system is of limited use. In situations when cases are scarce, a different representation scheme is called for, one that relies not on historical data for its inferencing but on available heuristics.

Rules often are used in situations in which the expert knows a domain well but has few recorded past cases to point to (a situation in which case-based reasoning would be impossible). Rule-based systems certainly are not limited to this type of application, but case-poor, heuristic-rich situations are where rule-based systems shine. One application in which this is evident is the diagnosis of private placement loans.

Private placement loans are negotiated between two parties (one party is usually a large financial services institution, the other an institution wishing to borrow) with neither party publicly requesting nor offering funds. Occasionally these loans go sour when the borrower gets into debt management trouble. Financial organizations that have made such loans that suddenly have a high probability of default look for another organization to take the loan off their hands *before* the borrower's financial troubles are widely known. Organizations involved in this game attempt to unload loans with a high probability of default and also try to avoid accepting souring loans that other companies are trying to unload. If the game is played well, the profits can be impressive. But a single default can flatten a year's profit margin.

The problem with prediction in this case is that there are few past case histories of private loan repudiation to draw upon. The number of private loans made by any one company is usually small and the number of defaults much smaller. Add to that the fact that institutions never advertise that one of the loans they've made has gone belly up. Few textbooks exist on underwriting private placement loans. And even the books that have been published cannot address problems or circumstances unique to one organization. So it becomes difficult to find information on past precedents for private loan default. Cases, then, are not suitable as a knowledge representation scheme in this situation.

In most lending institutions, however, there are experts in the recognition of failing loans. And their knowledge is usually available to the KE in the form of rules. The expert, for example, may suggest that the way to view bad loan prediction is as a series of symptoms that have causes and a series of causes that have cures. If a borrower has a particular symptom, then a certain set of causes must be behind that symptom. And if the cause of the symptom is known, but the borrowing institution has shown no interest in taking the cure, then the likelihood of loan default becomes too great to allow retention of the loan.

Rules in an expert system using this kind of "disease model" for diagnosis would encapsulate symptoms and causes, causes and then cures, or all three together in the same rule. A symptom-cause rule, for example, would focus on a company's debt-to-book ratio as an indicator of company financial health. (Debt-to-book ratio is a company's total liabilities or total long-term debt divided by the net asset value of its securities—essentially how much the company owes over how much it is worth.) A rapidly rising debt-to-book ratio may indicate that a company is piling up debt, which may point to loan repayment trouble later on. A rule to investigate this possibility would say (FQ stands for fiscal quarter):

IF symptom: debt-to-book this FQ/debt-to-book this FQ last year is greater than 1.1
THEN cause: company is taking on debt rapidly

(Translation: If this fiscal quarter's debt-to-book ratio is more than 10% greater than the ratio for the same time period last year, then the company is increasing its debt load more than 10% a year, that is, rapidly.)

The corollary cause-cure rule would say:

IF cause: company is taking on debt rapidly
THEN cure: sell certain assets
OR cure: reduce expenses
OR cure: raise product prices

An expert system designed in this way will analyze a borrowing company and, at the end of its considerations, list any symptoms identified for that company, along with any causes it has inferred from the symptoms and any suggestions for cures. It will then ask the user if any of the cures have been enacted by the ill company. If the answer is no, the system will offer recommendations for action (including recommending that the loan be sold to some other lender, presumably a lender who doesn't have access to a diagnostic expert system). In that way, souring loans will be dealt with before the loans become obvious problems.

This manner of rule formatting is not the only way of approaching the problem. The task might be looked at as a matter of selection and culling, rather than of disease diagnosis.

In a selection approach, rules would filter all the companies in a private placement loan portfolio, sift through the borrowers, and search for potential deadbeats. Rules in such a system would act as constraints, restricting the inclusion of companies in the portfolio into the "acceptable risk" subset and culling out companies that could not stand up to careful scrutiny.

The rulebase for this system would consist of a series of constraint rules that would give a "yea" or a "nay" to each company as that company passed before it for consideration. The rules would also tack a "Warning: Watch this company" rider on a potentially troublesome company. At the end of system execution, the companies in the portfolio would be displayed in ranked order according to their financial health, and any warning riders would be explained by the system. For example, a selection/culling rule would say

IF *company-x* debt-to-book this FQ / debt-to-book this FQ last year is greater than 1.1
THEN *company-x* warning explanation = "Company is taking on debt rapidly"
AND severity of problem = .7 + [(*company-x* debt-to-book this FQ / debt-to-book this FQ last year) -1.1]
AND *company-x* Warning counter = *company-x* Warning counter + (1 x severity of problem)
AND *company-x* check = "Check for large stock buyback as reason for ratio rise"
AND *company-x* check = "Check for personnel/growth imbalance"

(Translation: If this quarter's debt-to-book ratio is more than 10% greater than the ratio for the same time period last year for this particular company, then attach a brief explanation of the debt problem to that company's expert system-generated file under the heading of "Warning explanation." The debt-to-book ratio is usually a problem of severity .7 (on a 0 to 1.0 scale). But the severity of the problem increases as the amount of debt rises. So any rise of more than 10% in the debt-to-book will increase the perceived severity of the problem.

The severity of this problem, and any other problems the system discovers with this company, will all be tallied in the company's file under "Warning counter." And possible causes of the rapid debt-to-book rise are placed in the file under "Check." In this case, a rapid rise in the ratio may mean the company did not actually incur more debt, but bought back its own stock, that is, it reduced the denominator of the ratio rather than raising the numerator. Or the company may have anticipated more growth than it got and so took on too many people too quickly, an occasional problem with fast-growing companies.)

With this method, companies would be filtered through the system. Those with a warning counter of 0 would be placed in the acceptable risk pool. Those with a warning counter more than 0 would be ranked according to their likelihood of imminent default. (Ranking the companies could be done with just pencil and paper as a simple checklist. No AI is involved in this task.)

A prototype system would explain why particular warnings were given for each company by spilling the warning explanation file for that company. And it would offer recommendations for further investigation of the company by spilling the check file.

In a more advanced system, the investigations of warnings and checks would not be left up to the user. The system itself would make note of the warning explanations and checks. Then it would investigate (via rules) the borrowing company's on-line balance sheet, income statement, and credit reports and look for valid reasons the company may have had for raising its debt-to-book ratio. Such a system would not only rate a company's risk, but also investigate and explain any extenuating circumstances for increases in that risk.

Examples of the constraint types that the selection/culling system would use follow:

Positive requisition

>   IF X is present, THEN Y must be present also

Negation

>   IF X is not present, THEN Y must be present

Positive contingency

>   IF X occurs, THEN Y must occur before or after

Substitution

>   IF X is needed, THEN Y or Z may be substituted

Positive implication

>   IF X is present, THEN Y should also be present

Negative implication

>   IF X is present, THEN Y should not be present

Positive exclusion

>   IF X is present, THEN Y must not be present

Negative exclusion

>   IF X is not present, THEN Y must not be present

Positive limitation

IF X is present, THEN Y must not be larger than Z

Negative limitation

IF X is not present, THEN Y must not be larger than Z

Positive conjunction

IF X and Y, THEN Z

Positive disjunction

IF X or Y, THEN Z

Negative disjunction

IF X or Y, THEN not Z

Disjunctive negation

IF no X nor Y, THEN Z

Negative disjunctive negation

IF no X nor Y, THEN not Z

Private placement loan analysis need not be done by in-depth selection and culling, though. The simplest system, perhaps a suitable first prototype, would be daemon-based. A *daemon* is a rule that is invoked immediately and intrusively in a given circumstance as soon as its premises are satisfied. Usually daemons are used to warn the expert system user immediately of an undesirable situation (for example, equipment overheating in a process control application). In the private placement loan case, daemons would fire as soon as they noticed an incipient problem with a borrowing company. Time would not be a critical factor in the system since the loan portfolio would be reviewed only on a weekly basis at most. But daemons could reveal to the user (by posting warnings on the screen) the expert system's thought processes immediately after the user had answered a question. Such a system can show first-time users what the system is thinking as it considers the private borrowers.

Frames

Daemons can also be used in another way, outside of entirely rule-based systems. They can be installed in the slot of a frame and executed to instantiate a value into that slot. In fact, daemons are most often used in largely frame-based systems.

It is easiest to conceptualize frames as index cards in a cabinet drawer. Each index card has inscribed in its top left corner a heading, for example, MODEL NUMBER. This heading is known as the *key slot*. Beneath the key slot are other subsidiary *slots*, which describe or expand on the key slot, for example,

MODEL NUMBER:

MODEL NAME:

MODEL TYPE:

SUBCOMPONENTS:

TANDEMS (other equipment usually used with this model):

PRICE:

In each frame, that is, on each card in the file, the expert system can *instantiate* values, that is, fill in data, into any of the frame's slots. Examples would be:

MODEL NUMBER: 8000BC

MODEL NAME: Flntmbl

MODEL TYPE: Pedimotor

SUBCOMPONENTS: 2483FRD, 7767BRNI

TANDEMS: Flntst-N Selector, Rbbl-3 Interconnect

PRICE: 1560.00

There may be thousands of frames in the file, but the value in each key slot will be unique. For example, only one frame in the file will have the model number 8000BC.

Each frame can lead the expert system to other MODEL NUMBER frames or to frames with different key slots. A frame-based system is likely to derive information from a variety of frames in order to perform a task. For instance, say we are a manufacturer of electronic equipment and have discovered a flaw in all our equipment that operates at a frequency of 0809512.5 kHz. We want to find out which sub-components of our equipment operate at that problem frequency. The problem may reside in only one type of subcomponent built into all the failing pieces of equipment. The system will have to study a great many frames to see which models use which subcomponents and at which frequencies each subcomponent operates. Eventually we can ferret out whether one particular subcomponent is causing all the faults. To do this, we ask the expert system to find all of the models that use a subcomponent that operates at the problem frequency of 0809512.5 kHz.

The expert system finds all the frames in which frequencies are listed. And it selects any subcomponent frames with our requested frequency in it, for example:

SUBCOMPONENT: 5554Blwnkl

FREQUENCIES: 0809512.5, 0809587.5, 0809587

MODEL TYPE: Prestidigitation facilitator

SUPPLIER: Rokt-J-Skwrl Inc.

ADDRESS: 512 Disk Drive, Kluge City, AK

The system then notes the subcomponent number in the key slot (5554Blwnkl) and finds any models that contain that subcomponent.

MODEL NUMBER: 2100AD

MODEL NAME: JTSN-3

MODEL TYPE: Rastro Ledgerdemain prestidigitator

SUBCOMPONENTS: Lroy-2, Jain-7, 5554Blwnkl

TANDEMS: Rokay-Rorge Phone Interconnect

PRICE: 2460.00

The system can then answer our request. It will tell us that model number 2100AD is one of the models that uses a subcomponent that operates at frequency 0809512.5 kHz.

In this application, SUBCOMPONENT: 5554Blwnkl *inherits* information from the MODEL NUMBER: 2100AD frame, that is, nowhere in the SUBCOMPONENT: 5554Blwnkl frame does it say that SUB-COMPONENT: 5554Blwnkl is used in model number 2100AD. That information has to be inherited down from the MODEL NUMBER: 2100AD frame.

This method of storing information in an *inheritance hierarchy* saves the KE from storing data redundantly. Data can be stored once in a single frame and then inherited by other frames that need the data.

This particular kind of application, in which subassemblies inherit from larger structures (a field called group technology among manu-facturers), is an ideal use of frame-based reasoning. Knowledge in such a system is already packaged into discrete quantities (models and subcomponents). And the people who use the knowledge have often tried to package it into databases in order to keep it organized.

One feature that a frame-based expert system offers over a database is the ability to store not only data but also procedures in a frame's slot. A frame differs from a database record or relation in that it can be instantiated with data in three different ways: by inheritance from another frame, by assignment from a user program, and by procedure (daemon).

A frame can have data *assigned* to it. For example, when the system asks, "How much do you want to spend on the model you are ordering?" and the user types "less than $1000.00," the system assigns $1000 to the frame slot USER PRICE LIMIT.

A frame can also *inherit* data from another frame that contains data about the category the frame falls into (a class), from another object in its class, or from a subobject containing information about sub-components of the object, for example:

A class

- ENERGY SOURCES: Alternative energy
- BENEFIT: Nonpolluting
- DEVICES: Solar, eolic, cogeneration, efficiency

An object in the class ENERGY SOURCES: Alternative energy

- DEVICE: Solar
- INSTALLATION: At point of use
- TYPE OF POWER GENERATION: Photovoltaics, passive design/thermal mass

An object in the class DEVICE: Solar

- TYPE OF POWER GENERATION: Photovoltaics
- MAINTENANCE: No moving parts
- PHOTOVOLTAIC COMPONENTS: Amorphous silicon sheet, metal framing

A subobject of the object TYPE OF POWER GENERATION: Photovoltaics

- PHOTOVOLTAIC COMPONENT: Amorphous silicon sheet
- PROCESSING: Continuous process pouring

In this example, if the system were asked, "What is the benefit of photovoltaics?" the TYPE OF POWER GENERATION: Photovoltaics frame would inherit Solar from the DEVICE frame, and DEVICE: Solar would inherit BENEFIT: Non-polluting from the ENERGY SOURCES: Alternative energy frame. If the system were then asked, "How are the parts of a photovoltaic cell made?" it would dip into PHOTOVOL-TAIC COMPONENTS: Amorphous silicon sheet to tell us that continuous process pouring was the method used for creating amorphous silicon. (Notice that classes often have an *is-a* relationship with their objects: A photovoltaic cell *is-a* solar device, solar *is-a* form of alternative energy. Subobjects and subclasses often have a *has-a* relationship with their objects and classes: A photovoltaic cell *has-a* component called an amorphous silicon sheet.)

A frame can also derive data (instantiate a slot) by invoking a procedure, such as a rule. For example:

TYPE OF POWER GENERATION: Photovoltaics

- MAINTENANCE: No moving parts
- PHOTOVOLTAIC COMPONENTS: Amorphous silicon sheet, metal framing
- SIZE OF SYSTEM NECESSARY: IF system is for single-family dwelling AND there are X people in the family THEN (Y kW x X) = system capacity

In this case, a procedure detailing *how to calculate* the data, rather than the data *themselves*, is listed under SIZE OF SYSTEM NECESSARY. In this way, not only can variable data be "attached" to each frame, but any warnings, cautions, hints, suggestions about assemblage, or advice can be made part of the frame. For example, a model number frame could say

MODEL NUMBER: 111111

MODEL NAME: RNDM

CONTINGENCIES: IF model-operation-frequency is less than 0809512.5 mHz, THEN finished-model must also contain component 432.2L to control amplitude modulation

Other Representation Schemes

Frames and rules are the two representation schemes used most often. But variations of frames and rules are also used in the development of expert system applications, including object-value pairs, object-attribute-value triplets, semantic nets, and logic.

Object-Value Pairs

Object-value (O-V) pairs are seldom used except when enforced by the limitations of a primitive development tool. O-V pairs structure the data and the relationships between the data into a simple two-part representation. The first part, the object, usually denotes a thing or an occurrence. The second part, the value, describes or expands on the thing or the occurrence. For example,

---

Position of circuit board #4476 / In third slot of motherboard

Place of manufacture of board #4476 / Kluge City, AK

The limitation of this scheme is that it makes dealing with many thousands of objects onerous and variable handling difficult. For example, in the O-V pairs above, it would be hard for a KE to ask the system to give the part numbers of all circuit boards installed in the motherboard's third slot which have been made in Kluge City, Alaska.

The KE could not write:

IF *board number x* has position of circuit board "in
third slot of motherboard"
AND *board number x* has place of manufacture "Kluge
City, AK"
THEN ...

but would have to address every object individually by saying

IF position of circuit board #1 is "in third slot of motherboard"
AND place of manufacture of board #1 is "Kluge City, AK"
THEN ...

IF position of circuit board #2 is "in third slot of motherboard"
AND place of manufacture of board #2 is "Kluge City, AK"
THEN ...

IF ...

If there are only a dozen board numbers, this is no problem. But if there are four million different board numbers, it would require four million separate rules (or four million premises in one rule) to make one inference.

Object-Attribute-Value Triplets

Object-attribute-value (O-A-V) triplets solve the variable-handling problem of O-V pairs by dividing the data into three pieces, each of which can be looked at independently, for example,

board #4476 / position / in third slot of motherboard

board #4476 / place of manufacture / Kluge City, AK

For this reason, the simplest premises and conclusions of most rules are usually written as O-A-V triplets, for example,

IF (currency trading-volume high)

or

IF currency.trading-volume high

(When the number of attributes and values for the same object increases, that is, when there are many attributes and values for one object, the knowledge representation scheme begins to resemble a frame with many attribute slots and value instantiations.)

Semantic Nets

Semantic nets are webs of association. They consist of *nodes* and *linkages* which express the relationships between nodes. Nodes come in two types: *objects* are usually things, and *descriptors* are usually events or descriptions of things. For example, in the following semantic net,"steam turbine," "turbine blade," and "cavitation" are objects. "Malfunction," "fracture," and "excess oxygen in steam" are descriptors. And "has-a" and "may be caused by" are linkages.

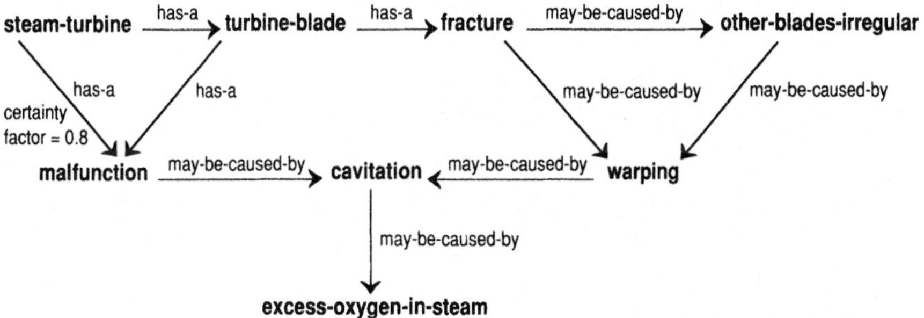

Semantic nets are often written in programming languages simply as frames in which certain slots are used to store the relationship between two or more other frames. This allows the storage of complex relationships in a straightforward format, for example:

ENGINE NUMBER: 2
LINK: has-a
DESCRIPTOR: Malfunction

ENGINE NUMBER: 2
LINK: has-a
OBJECT: Turbine blade

SUBCOMPONENT: Turbine blade
LINK: has-a
DESCRIPTOR: Fracture

Most languages that use logic as their representation scheme, for example, Prolog (PROgramming in LOGic), express data in the form of "sentences" called *predicate clauses* or *assertions*. Such clauses often present a relationship between items (the predicate) and then list the items themselves (objects), for example:

Component-of (CPU, computer)

Component-of (ALU, CPU)

Component-of (IC, ALU)

(Translation: A CPU (central processing unit) is a component of a computer. An ALU (arithmetic logic unit) is a component of a CPU. An IC (integrated circuit) is a component of an ALU.)

?- Component-of (A, computer)

A = CPU

?- Component-of (B, CPU)

B = ALU

?- Component-of (C, ALU)

C = IC

?- Component-of (X, Component-of (Y, Component-of (Z, Computer)))

X = IC

Y = ALU

Z = CPU

(Translation: What is a component of a Computer? A CPU. What is a component of a CPU? An ALU. What is a component of an ALU? An IC. What is a component of whatever is a component of the component of a computer? An IC is a component of an ALU, which is a component of a CPU, which is a component of a computer.)

Logic allows a KE to just present items and state the relationships between them. Then the logic language's own inference engine sorts out the various relationships between the items (as it did above: inferring that an IC is a component of a computer because an IC is a component of an ALU, and an ALU is a component of a CPU, which is a component of a computer).

Many of logic programming's proponents hold that logic is the cleanest, most lucid, most succinct form in which to represent knowl-

---

edge. And logic is often used in applications in which the relationship between things is paramount, such as natural language sentence morphology (subject, predicate, modifier, etc.). But logic's detractors hold that because logic languages are so entirely declarative (statement oriented), it is difficult to handle procedural tasks (what to do with relationships once they've been discovered) or to build hybrid systems using logic alone.

Costing, Metrics, and Specification   8

The Knowledge Engineer as Accountant

From a business perspective, cost projection may be the first concern of anyone considering the development of an expert system. In any corporate environment, cost considerations clearly will carry substantial weight, often becoming the salient criterion on which the decision to develop an expert system is made. Cost estimation, then, becomes one of the concerns for a knowledge engineer.

Ordinarily the initial approach to a problem is to isolate the stages of system development and the constraints that will affect project costs. From a distance, development, implementation, and maintenance appear as the larger stages, but within each stage are further divisions. In fact, cost concerns span all levels of system construction.

The phases of expert system development that can be anticipated in most scenarios include the following:

- prospecting

- knowledge acquisition

- knowledge representation

- coding

- tool development (sometimes) before the expert system itself is built

- integration of the expert system with other systems

- training

The most common expert system development costing factors include expenses, savings, and maintenance.

Expenses

Personnel Costs

Personnel costs include the following items:

- cost of KEs (depending on skill/experience)

- costs to train KEs, users, managers

- domain expert availability (cost of the domain expert's consultation time during the project)

- travel and ancillary costs

Knowledge-Based Costs

Knowledge-based costs are the costs of fulfilling the expert system's hardware and software requirements. These costs depend on the following items:

- cost of new hardware/software for expert system development

- knowledgebase volume and complexity (the number of discrete knowledge processes, islands, chunks, tasks, rules, and frames incorporated into the knowledgebase and their size and sophistication)

- amount of prospecting, knowledge acquisition, knowledge representation, and coding needed to complete the system

- amount of knowledge encoded at present (textbooks, manuals, and scribbled notes)

- cost associated with the role/purpose of the expert system in the organization and, consequently, the time needed to build it (the cost of building an advisory vs. a proxy vs. a backend vs. a consultancy vs. a tutorial system)

- failure tolerance needs (the severity of the consequences if an expert system offers faulty or incomplete advice, which affects the amount of testing the expert system must undergo before being fielded)

- future genericization/extrapolation of application (the cost of coding one expert system so it can be expanded later into other systems, or "genericized"; made into a tool)

- meta-level knowledge requirements (the costs of discovering and coding meta-level knowledge, which is knowledge about how to manipulate the knowledge in the knowledgebase—most important in tutorial applications)

- cooperation of expert systems (costs of ensuring commonality between systems—usually via blackboards—so they can talk to each other)

Tool Costs

Tool costs are based on the following factors:

- tool-level requirements (the cost/need for a certain language or development tool)

- tool-development costs (the cost of gutting a similar expert system to provide a skeleton for a system under consideration or of developing a tool from scratch)

- integration costs (the cost of linkage to existing systems)
  - linking expert system hardware to conventional hardware
  - linking expert system software to conventional software (DP, MIS, DSS)
  - linking the expert system to existing databases
  - linking the expert system to newly created (custom) databases (written in the expert system's language)
  - linking the expert system to programs working in other AI disciplines (natural language translation, robotics, CAD, image analysis)

Savings

Personnel Savings

Savings incurred as a result of the reduction of people/time involved in given tasks because of the expert system's use are contingent on the following particulars:

- the number of domain experts reduced or the time of domain experts saved as a result of the new expert system (savings in salaries, office space, training, downtime)

- increased domain expert productivity and increased complexity of work handled as a result of downloading routine decisions to the expert system

- increased profitability of the organization as a result of previously unavailable expertise now being distributed via the expert system

- savings in travel and ancillary costs (of users, programmers, experts, and managers) as a result of the expert system's implementation

Knowledge-Based Savings

Knowledge-based savings are based on the following aspects:

- value of the strategic edge conferred on the organization as the result of one expert system's development or of the organization's ability to develop expert systems in-house

- increased organizational profitability/productivity as the result of the expert system (reduction of workload, reduction in time unproductively spent seeking answers from experts, value of opportunities previously lost until the expert system was made available, increased customer and employee satisfaction)

- value (present and future) to the organization of trained knowledge engineers/users/managers

- value to the organization of knowledge previously never codified and now collected in one place (and no longer able to just walk out the door with the domain expert)

- savings of using the expert system as a domain expert backup or proxy

- autonomy scale savings (savings as a result of reduced human intervention in problem solution)

- future genericization/extrapolation savings (decreased costs of building future expert systems as a result of experience gained in building this one)

Tool Savings

Tool savings are contingent on the following items:

- savings of the cost of conventional hardware/software that was not developed/purchased because the expert system made it unnecessary

---

- savings in development time for future applications as a result of having a guttable expert system that might be used as a shell in the future

- value of shells and genericized tools created in a project and salable within or outside an organization

Integration

The savings incurred by integrating the expert system with other programs are dependent on the value of the linkage to other hardwares, systems, databases, expert systems, or conventional programs made as a result of building the expert system.

Maintenance

The amount of maintenance (and the cost of maintenance) of an expert system generally depends on four factors:

- The validity of the original design (the need to revise an inference engine or knowledgebase after the system has been delivered to the users) will influence the amount of time spent overhauling a system to bring it into conformity with user needs, which may change over time.

- The volatility of the domain knowledge (the need to add, modify, or delete parts of the expert system's knowledgebase because knowledge in the domain has changed) will influence the amount of time spent cleaning, tuning, building up, or paring down a knowledgebase.

- Integration between the expert system and other systems will act as a multiplying factor when changes to the expert system are needed, because a change to the knowledgebase may affect the way in which data are collected from other systems (say, an external database) or the format in which data are stored or handed to another system. The ripples of change to other systems caused by a change to an expert system will add maintenance costs.

- The transfer of knowledge about the expert system's code will result in training costs for new KEs being taught to maintain the expert system, for example, the costs of preparing documentation of the knowledgebase (in some cases, documentation of each rule or frame in the system) to assist new KEs in learning about the expert system.

Iterative Specification and Metrics

Iterative specification is an attempt to eliminate padding and intuitive stumbling toward success. A method of specification that considers the unique requisites of expert system prototyping, it requires that:

- specification be done in phases

- these regular periods of reassessment be incorporated into the project management process

- some form of formal description (for example, deciding what will constitute success) be agreed upon at each phase

- the metrics used to judge project success and completion be regularly reanalyzed and updated

- notes be diligently compiled on each phase of project progress (costs, schedules, coding requirements, risks, project depth and breadth) to make true projection (not just estimation) possible on future projects

Under the iterative specification method, a project is routinely reviewed for both compliance with past specs and the creation of future metrics. Resources, dimensions, and workmanship are all scrutinized, and which aspect of the project to concentrate on (or, in fact, whether to go on with the project at all) is determined during each review period. Iterative specification is also useful in deciding exactly when the project will be considered completed.

There are two ways of delineating the phases of iterative specification: the temporal method and the task method. Most organizations will use both approaches at some point in the prototyping/specification process.

Temporal reviews are those held on a regular basis: every week, every month, every quarter. All of a project's various aspects may be discussed at a temporal review. And such a process usually yields the best idea of a project's overall health. The advantage of temporal reviews is that they provide an integrated picture of all the project's pieces and the interconnections between those pieces.

Task reviews are held only upon completion of a particular task or upon realization of a severe problem with that task. Task reviews may be accomplished by oral or written report or brief meetings with project managers. Their purpose is to determine whether a specific function has been fulfilled by a portion of the expert system. The advantage of task reviews is that they provide a clear picture of each piece of the larger system.

Both temporal and task reviews are part of the ongoing and iterative formal description process necessitated by the prototyping approach. They can be thought of as performance/design reviews. And, because they are used to define deliverables (what the users will receive), all reviews should answer three questions:

- What has been done to bring the project nearer to successful completion?

- What is being done at the moment?

- What needs to be done (especially during the current phase of development)?

Within the iterative specification methodology, metrics are created and results measured by means of a variety of design/performance reviews. Each type of review is meant to assess the progress of a particular aspect of the developing expert system.

The Procedural Review

Procedural reviews assess the *behavior* of an expert system in any given phase of its development, including the following aspects:

- the program's lucidity (the ability of naive users to understand the questions it asks and the directions it offers)

- the program's ability to explain itself (through explanation mechanisms) both to the KE (during development) and to the users (during actual use)

- the validity of the conclusions and advice given by the expert system

A review committee may include representatives from all groups affected by development of the expert system. The domain expert may be asked, "Is this prototype's approach to problem solution valid? Do the facts, suppositions, conclusions, and inferences made by the expert system prototype appear to be correct?" The user may be asked, "Is this expert system, as it stands, of help to you in the performance of your job? What should be added/modified/deleted to make the system do what you need it to do?" The project manager may be asked, "Is the progress made so far acceptable? Is there an area of greater strategic advantage or immediate value to the organization that should be concentrated on?" And the KE may be asked, "What has been completed since the last review? What difficulties do you foresee? What do you need to complete this phase of development?"

The ideal procedural review committee will take care to focus on larger system functionality issues and not be too concerned about the expert system's "flash" (user-interface features known in MIS as "bells and whistles"). The principal concerns should always be whether this system does what it was built to do and what the users need it to do.

The Technical Review

A technical review is most likely to involve a presentation by the KE describing the headway made in solving technical problems, including an examination of the following items:

- newly encountered "challenges" (difficulties), especially when those challenges were unanticipated in the original conception of the system

- the suitability of the tools being used, if the project is still in its early stages

- the feasibility of designing certain features into the expert system (new features requested by users becoming comfortable with the expert system's capabilities)

- the control flow and data flow, the system's adherence to some type of structured programming requirements, its documentation, and its input/output requirements

- the validity of the expert system and the efficiency of its methods of inference, inheritance, and knowledge representation (for example, redundant rules, omitted objects, incomplete semantic nets)

Users may ask, "Can this feature be built into the expert system? If not, can a suitable substitute be devised?" The project manager may ask, "What tools/languages/linkages/training/technical personnel will be needed to complete the project?"

The Position Review

Position reviews are often conferences between users and KEs. Their purpose is to determine how the expert system will fit into an organization. (In a sense, position reviews are a continuation of the prospecting configuration process.)

- Users and KEs determine which user group will adopt the expert system as its own.

- They determine who in the group will use the system and how using it will affect the role of the domain expert for that group.

- They may decide when part of the completed system can be "frozen" and given to users for testing or implementation.

- If it is possible to segment the expert system into separately functional subsystems or to build the expert system in layers, each one useful on its own, the position review is the time to draw boundaries around the usable subsystems, so they can be finished and transferred to users as soon as possible.

Other Reviews

- *The expansion review* determines whether to continue or halt development, expand to new areas, or prune the current system.

- *The integration review* analyzes the process of making linkages, and coordinating input/output between the expert system and other systems.

- *The personnel review* looks at who is involved, when, and for how long.

- *The ancillary reviews* examine knowledgebase security, fault tolerance, system autonomy, and so on.

- *The human factors review* determines whether the interface meets the needs of the users.

The review process is far more flexible in practice than might be imagined from the preceding descriptions. Organizations differ in the amount of management they will accept. Corporate cultures will dictate how the iterative specification process will actually work on a particular project. KEs in some organizations will fulfill certain review requirements with each member of the development team (domain expert, user, manager) individually and informally. Others will prefer to assemble all parties for monthly status assessments, in which different reviews are incorporated. And some will perform task reviews whenever necessary and with whoever is available, and also prepare reports for monthly/quarterly temporal reviews to keep manangement abreast of project developments.

Pages from a Knowledge Engineer's Notebook:
An Iterative Specification Review Checklist and
Specific Questions to Answer During the Review Process

Procedural Review

- lucidity of questions the expert system asks
- lucidity of directions the expert system gives
- validity of conclusions and advice the system offers
- system's explanations to KEs
- system's explanations to users

Technical Review

- technical hurdles leapt
- new hurdles
- suitability of tools
- feasibility of new features
- control flow structure
- data flow
- documentation
- validity/efficiency of inference method
- validity/efficiency of inheritance method
- validity/efficiency of representation schemes

Position Review

- Who will adopt (maintain) the finished expert system?
- Who will use it?
- When will the next version be frozen?
- When will the project be completed?
- How long before the system is useful and usable?
- How much will it cost?
- What is the project life cycle (for example, prospecting, prototyping, implementation, transfer to users)?

Costing, Metrics, and Specification

- What will the dimensions of the system be (how many rules, frames, etc.)?

- How many people will be required to work on the project and for how long?

- What will their roles be?

- Which languages, tools, and linkages to other files or programs will be necessary for the completion of the project?

- How much time will be required of the domain expert, KE, and users?

Knowledge Engineering Techniques   *9*

The Knowledge Engineer as Programmer

Expert system code may be changed daily for many months or years while a system is under development. It is the *expectation* of this constant change, growth, and flexibility that has resulted in the development of certain software engineering techniques unique to commercial AI.

This chapter examines many of the programming and expert system management techniques employed by KEs working in commercial AI. These methods often have evolved as a result of the unique demands of the expert system development process.

Expansion Journals

Expansion journals are files used to collect user suggestions for the expansion of an expert system. They can be thought of as the first step in automating the knowledge acquisition process.

Expansion journals usually are implemented by providing users with a command callable from anywhere in the expert system, such as Opinion, Comment, or Question. The user can then give this command to create a separate window in a corner of the screen that collects comments and suggestions.

Expansion journals allow the user to do the following:

- propose vocabulary that should be defined in later revisions of the system

- identify confusing questions or incomplete responses given by the expert system

- point out where the system makes incorrect assumptions or draws improper conclusions

- request improvements in the system's depth or breadth of knowledge

Users and domain experts type in their comments while they are working with the system; later the KE acts on their remarks. Thus, users can make suggestions on improving or expanding the system directly into the expansion journal without the KEs having to hover over them. This approach frees the KE from having to be present whenever the system is run, allowing experts and users to go through and comment on the expert system at their own convenience.

Examples of expansion journal comments may include such user observations as follow:

"The seventh question the expert system asks does not make sense. It should say...."

"The six answers the system gives me to choose from in question 26 don't include the answer I want to give, which is...."

"Question 33 allows me to give only one answer. But I need to give two answers to that question."

"Question 9 should not have come up. The system should not have to ask me this. It should have inferred it from my answer to the previous question."

A more advanced journal will attach a time/date/user tag to a user's comment, along with a note labeling which expert system question the user is looking at, so the user need only say, "This question is not right," rather than "Question 61C is not right."

Expansion journals are a technique for guiding the progress of expert system development according to the needs of the system's users and experts. Journals allow users to propose the path of expansion. And the KE need not try to anticipate or guess the users' needs.

Expansion Logs

Expansion logs are files used to record the path a user takes when using the expert system. Their principal purpose is to reveal to the KE which parts of the system are being used most often and how. This information will allow the KE to focus development of the system on areas that are getting the most use.

An expansion log may record, for example, the following items:

- questions asked by the expert system during an execution session

- responses made by the user to each question

- rules fired during system execution or which rules have been found to be true or false

- frame slots instantiated (for example, "125 was instantiated into the slot yen-value in the frame dollar")

- hypotheses the rules were trying to prove at each step in the session

- cases that have been looked at during the session (in case-based systems)

- recommendations or actions made by the expert system

- data removed from or placed in external databases or the information handed to conventional programs integrated with the expert system

- how often certain parts of the expert system were called into play during a particular session.

Implementing an expansion log may be as simple as just starting a trace or a log (a utility of this sort usually is provided as a component of an AI language or tool) before a session. Or it may involve rigging a method of capturing particular kinds of expert system usage data (such as recording how frequently certain rules fire). It may even involve creating a graphical representation of the knowledgebase and color coding it to highlight the parts of the system that get the most use.

Expansion logs differ from expansion journals not only in their purpose but in how users interact with them. An expansion *journal* allows users to contribute directly to the system's refinement and growth by making suggestions to a file read by the KE. An expansion *log* is created by the system itself, without any effort on the user's part.

The user may throw a switch to begin recording the execution session or to stop it. But other than that, direct user input into the log is not necessary and, often, not allowed.

Expansion logs have several uses. They can, for instance, be employed as a reference by the expert system user. When an expert system session is long and complex or likely to be interrupted, an expansion log (which can be printed out or dislayed on the screen during the session) will be of help to a user trying to remember which questions have already been asked and which answers/advice the system has already given. Such an expansion log would be likely to include the questions asked by the system, the answers given by the user, and the conclusions drawn by the system along the way. It would not include the firing of rules or the instantiation of frame slots.

When a final decision has been made by the user, an expansion log can even be preserved in hard copy to show that the user acted in accordance with the recommendations of the expert system. More often, the expansion log is studied by the KE. When prototypes are being debugged, a list of system "reactions and responses" can help the KE identify the system's thought processes. The programmer, trudging back through reams of log printout, can often identify where an expert system began to make incorrect assumptions or to offer improper advice.

The principal use of an expansion log is to guide an expert system's expansion by recording the "movements" of users through the system. When debugging is finished and the first-stage system is being used, KEs use the logs to decide where future development of the expert system should be concentrated. Such an expansion log may record the frequency with which certain rules are invoked (over the course of *many* sessions with *many* users) or the route that users typically take while wending through an expert system's series of questions (which may point out inefficiencies in coding).

Any part of the expert system that the expansion log shows is seldom used may become a lower priority for expansion than one that is used all the time. The expansion log thereby saves future time and development effort by showing which parts of the expert system users turn to most often.

Blackboards

Broadly speaking, blackboards (also called erasable contexts, scratchpads, or scribble memory) are temporary files in which data, facts, beliefs, and relationships are stored during program execution. They often appear only during system execution and then disappear after a program has finished. Blackboards have two different purposes, depending on where they are employed:

- They can be used to facilitate the exchange of information between the parts of an expert system.

- They can be used to help transfer information between expert systems and other programs or databases.

These different purposes, however, make use of the same general architecture. Blackboards are holding pens; they act as the communication mechanism between two programs or two parts of a program that are communicating with each other. When one part has information, it writes that information onto the blackboard. When the other part needs that information, it retrieves the information from the blackboard. In this way, the two parts need not be directly linked to each other to exchange information, and they need not suspend their execution, waiting until the other part is ready to accept the information.

Blackboards, then, hold information that is to be conveyed between expert and conventional systems, or they act as temporary stores of data within single multi-faceted expert systems whose different components must communicate with each other.

In a sense, blackboards provide a kind of short-term communal memory shared between expert system components or between expert and conventional systems. Their benefit is that they allow a greater measure of control and manageability over the data communications task, and they often increase the speed and efficiency of the expert system. They do not, for example, require that a conventional program wait before giving information to an expert system. They allow the expert system and the conventional program to work at their own tasks independently, providing information to each other via the blackboard when they have data available and retrieving data from the blackboard when necessary. This approach can increase performance speeds when the expert system is dealing with such external sources of data as livefeeds from stock-quotation retrieval services or process control feeds (pyrometers, tensiometers, moisture-meters), which convey the status of manufacturing machinery and ongoing processes.

Such a method, used in steel manufacture, for example, might allow the pyrometers to record in-furnace temperatures, show them on an operator's screen, and simultaneously post them to a blackboard every 30 seconds. The expert system may then monitor other factors in the manufacturing process and, when it detects an anomaly that could be temperature related, grab the *latest* pyrometer reading from the blackboard to make an inference. In this way, both the temperature measurement equipment and the expert system can work at their own pace, and also share data.

Blackboards also allow for the subdivision of programming tasks. One task is to write data onto the blackboard; another is to remove those data from the board. The KE, then, can solve software linkage (integration) problems in stages by dividing the job into two segments: 1) expert system transmittal and 2) database/conventional-program retrieval.

Blackboards permit the KE to begin the expert system as a standalone without first having to solve the entire linkage issue (which, in a large project, may require a year or more of effort). One KE can solve the problem of retrieving data from the blackboard first and put dummy data in the blackboard for expert system prototype testing while someone else works on the task of sending data from the conventional program to the blackboard.

This kind of indirect linkage through a blackboard allows data communications tasks to be modularized. One module in each conventional program passes input/output between the conventional programs and the blackboard. And one module in the expert system passes input/output between the blackboard and the expert system.

Blackboards can reduce the complexity of software integration problems, increase maintainability, and simplify the data communications task in large systems. And when used inside a single large expert system, they can make a program run more efficiently by allowing each part of the system to retrieve and post its information according to its own needs and timetable.

Designated Windowing

Designated windowing is not a technique created by KEs, but one that has been expropriated by them and put to good use. Designated windows are simply portions of a computer monitor's screen set aside to contain certain types of action or provide certain kinds of data to the user. Large expert systems (especially those monitoring complex engineering processes, financial markets, or control networks, such as urban automobile traffic or electrical power grids) often use this method to show all relevant data tables, graphs, and warnings/recommendations on the screen simultaneously.

For example, an expert system that uses designated windows may allow data updates on temperature to be bar-graphed in one corner, with expert system recommendations on temperature adjustment appearing in a banner beneath the graph: written in blue, they signal a minor change; in red, they recommend a major readjustment.

To the right of that window may be a box listing one-minute pressure measurements in a simple table format, with an expert system-created warning mechanism that beeps and flashes whenever the system has compared several dozen factors and discovered that their convergence may actuate a rapid drop in pressure.

Beneath that window may be a group of manipulable *icons* created and controlled by the expert system code. In this example, such icons could include a circular gauge with a centered rotating arm pointing to moisture-level readings in the gauge and a three-dimensional cup filled with liquid that rises and falls in depth showing the volume of material in a vat.

To the left of the icon area may be a pie chart that shows by differently colored segments the amounts of the various materials now being processed, with an arrow pointing to the pie segment (the material) the expert system has judged to be too scarce or too plentiful in the mix.

In the center of the screen may be a graphical representation that explains pictorially the entire process under study, with colors designating problems detected by the diagnostic expert system.

And tucked up in a far corner may be a window whose purpose is to utter what are sometimes referred to as *contentment calls*. These tell the screen viewer that the expert system is indeed up and running and that it is monitoring the process on a continuous basis and finding nothing untoward to report. Contentment calls may be presented in any of the following formats:

- a series of statements detailing which parts of the process are currently under study by the expert system, for example: "02:34:11:26 Taking pressure reading. 02:34:12:52 Taking temperature reading..."

- an all-encompassing statement delivered every ten seconds, for example: "Check of the process made at 10:22:23. No problems discovered. No adjustments necessary."

- a sliding-line graph, which looks like an EKG readout with the time written on top and which sends up sharp peaks ("heartbeats") at regular intervals.

Designated windows, then, allow a KE to present vast quantities of background information while making the expert system's recommendations known to the user and visually and auditorily highlighting important or urgent advice.

Graphical Decomposition

Graphical decomposition allows the expert system's input to be in the form of pictures (drawn, or fed in, by the user) rather than text. It allows a user to draw on the screen (using a mouse or a puck) or to scan in an image that is then studied by the expert system and decomposed into a form it can infer from: usually frames or O-A-V triplets. Raw data gleaned from such a picture may include the length or width of lines, their placement on a screen, their contiguity or intersection with other lines, the area of dark or light patches in the picture, or the ratio of objects recognized by the expert system.

A *drawn* picture may be, for example, the footprint of a building with the streets around it sketched in, the position of north designated, and entrances to the building noted. Such information could be used by a real estate evaluation expert system to determine the amount of sunshine a building is likely to receive (deduced from the position of north), the amount of congestion at the building's entrances (from the number of entrances and their placement), and traffic patterns (according to street positions). All of these factors would influence the value of the building (especially in a crowded city such as Tokyo).

Scanned images decomposed by an expert system may be, for example, digitized photographs of a glaucoma patient's eye. Glaucoma can cause the rupture of blood vessels in the eye, which can result in a loss of sight when oxygenated blood is no longer carried to the base of the optic nerve. Photographs of the fundus (the back of the eye) can reveal the amount of necrotic (dead) tissue in the optic disk (where the optic nerve exits the eye on its way to the brain's occipital lobe). Necrotic tissue is pale because nourishing blood does not reach it, whereas healthy tissue is rosy. A physician can compare an old photograph of a patient's fundus with a photograph of the same fundus taken six months after prescription of a drug to stop the hemorrhaging and can determine whether any more tissue has been damaged since the drug treatment began. But an expert system can detect the success or failure of drug treatment by analyzing pictures taken only days apart, rather than months. It does this by comparing the number of light and dark pixels (picture elements) on the photograph, deciding where the boundary is between healthy and necrotic tissue (edge detection), and calculating the area of the dead tissue in both photographs. This information on the progress or cessation of hemorrhaging then allows the expert system to readjust drug protocols for that particular patient.

Graphical decomposition allows an expert system to treat data that are not easily rendered into words. It does so by either providing an easier, more natural method of data input (architectural drawings rather than verbal descriptions of a building) or allowing the input of data that could not enter an expert system in any other format (realtime video freezeframes taken by a repair-and-maintenance submarine using an expert system to tell the sub where it is in relation to an underwater object it sees through its cameras).

Graphical Explanation

Graphical explanation is an expert system's way of explaining pictorially, rather than verbally, what it has concluded. Graphical explanation facilities convey a great deal of information to the user at a single glance.

The simplest graphical explanation facilities feature only a graph or a scanned image with superimposed arrows or fingers pointing to the part of the picture the user should attend to. An expert system advising a block equity trader to prepare for a downturn in stock price, for example, may put a graph of the stock's performance on the screen along with a highlighted 30-day moving average line and an arrow pointing to where the recent price has dropped just far enough below the trend line to suggest trouble ahead.

More complex graphical explanation facilities portray a process or an object in schematic form on the screen as the system is running. When the expert system diagnoses a problem in a jet engine or manufacturing equipment, for example, it highlights the areas on the schematic where the problem is likely to occur. It may brighten the color of the piece of equipment on the screen or flash the image of the faulty piece while announcing the problem, through a speech synthesizer, to a busy operator.

Enterprise Models and Iconographic Menus

Enterprise models are charts or schematics, drawn by a KE and put on the screen by the expert system, that show the way in which an organization or a process works. An enterprise model for a long-distance telecommunications network, for example, might show a picture of a customer's telephone linked to a building labeled "local telephone central office" linked to a transfer point labeled "point of presence" linked to "switches" and "data access points" and with arrows showing how a typical phone call negotiates its way through the network from the caller's phone to the receiver's phone. Such a model can convey to the user a good deal of information on the relationships among the different parts of a large process or organization. It can also serve as a useful user-interface to the expert system if it is used as an iconographic menu.

Iconographic menus ask questions of an expert system user by presenting "live" pictures. The user can mouse-click on a portion of the whole picture and call up information stored "behind" that part of the screen. A user might, for instance, click on the picture of the "point of presence." The expert system would then offer, in a separate window, an explanation of the purpose of points of presence in a telecomm network or ask the user questions relating to points of presence.

Iconographic menus work by storing blocks of data (objects) together with screen X-Y coordinate boundaries. When a user clicks on a part of the screen within those boundaries, the system displays whatever data the user requests about that icon or it initiates a process to gather those data. What the user sees is one large complex drawing, schematic, or map. But what the system recognizes is actually dozens (or hundreds) of separate fragments, each of which has data or procedures associated with it.

Iconographic menus are used in the following instances:

- as a form of *visual language* when the information being presented to the user (or the question being asked) would require reams of text if it were not presented graphically

- when the number of possible questions that could be asked of a user is large, and the KE would rather have the system display only one menu screen to (in a sense) ask all the questions at once

- when the KE wants the system to present information to the user at the same time that the system is asking its questions (as if to say, "This is how phone calls flow through a telecomm network. Now which part of this network would you like to know more about?" or "Which part is the portion you believe is causing the trouble?")

Dynamic Knowledgebases

Dynamic knowledgebases allow the user some flexibilty in deciding which factors will be important in an expert system's inferencing at a certain time. In effect, they allow the user to adjust the knowledgebase while the system is up and running.

An expert system that has a dynamic knowledgebase usually provides the user with a subsidiary window in a corner of the screen. In that window is a list of the factors whose importance the user can adjust. The user can move the factor indicators along a sliding scale, thereby establishing which factors the expert system should pay closest attention to.

An electric utility network diagnostic system, for example, might list a dozen general types of alarms that the system knows about (alarms caused when, for instance, a transformer is tampered with, or a high-tension wire snaps in a storm). When a network problem occurs that results in hundreds of different warning messages raining down into the expert system from the network, the user can adjust the dynamic knowledgebase to let the system know which types of messages to pay close attention to, which to downplay, and which to ignore. The user can do this by setting the indicator on the sliding scale beside each factor in the window according to how important he or she believes that factor is. By setting one type of alarm to low importance (by clicking on the sliding scale with a mouse), the user tells the system to discount those alarms in its analysis of the problem situation. By setting another type of alarm to high importance, the user instructs the system to weigh this factor heavily in any decisions on how to handle the overall problem.

Dynamic knowledgebases are often used for speculation (asking the expert system, "If these were the factors, what would you recommend?"). They also are often used in fields in which the user of the expert system is also the domain expert. In such cases, the expert may want more control over the system, in order to use it as a tool to clarify decision making rather than as an advisor to follow slavishly.

In such situations, the factors that influence a decision by the expert system are known beforehand, but not the degree to which those factors will influence a decision. Bond traders may, for example, know that the various elements of the consumer price index influence bond prices, but they may not know how much of an influence each factor will have at any given time. It is difficult, in that case, for a KE to write in rules that explicitly state the degree to which certain factors affect bond prices.

The knowledgebase, then, is made to be manipulated by the user. The expert system knows which factors will influence its decision. These are put in the dynamic knowledgebase window. The user then adjusts the factors to fit the immediate circumstances of a particular market. A bond trader may decide that the effect of lower housing starts this month will be negligible on bond prices and set that indicator low. But because of recent political events that the expert system could not be privy to, the trader may set the growth in the money supply to very important. Thus, a dynamic knowledgebase combines the best of a human expert's abilities (intuition) with the best of an expert system's abilities (sleeplessness, thoroughness, and the ability to consider many factors at once).

Explanation Facilities

The explanation facility is that part of an expert system that explains the following:

- why a question is being asked of the user

- what particular answers made by the expert system mean

- how to pursue a recommendation made by the expert system

- why a certain recommendation for action was made

Explanation facilities built into a tool or a language to assist in coding an expert system are usually "justifiers," which act by "backtracking." They tell the programmer which rule premises were found to be true and which data were gleaned from which frames, resulting in the firing of which rules. Because such backtracking is generally completely inscrutable to users, explanation facilities in finished expert systems usually are not tool created, but rather KE-created natural language fragments (blocks of English language text, for example).

Explanation text may spell out the following information:

- WHY: Why is this question being asked? What is the expert system trying to get at by asking the user this question? Why is the system giving this recommendation? What factors led it to believe that this is the right course of action?

- WHAT: What does that unfamiliar word used by the expert system mean? What does the answer given by the expert system imply?

- HOW, WHEN, WHERE, WHO: How is that action performed? When should the user commit the action recommended by the system to stop a problem from worsening? Where should the user look on a piece of machinery to find the problem? Which departments should be contacted when this situation occurs? Who should be notified of the action about to be taken?

Intelligent Deferral

In the early stages of an expert system's use—while it is undergoing it's first field trials—the recommendations a system gives may not be deemed acceptable by the user. The expert system may not yet know everything it should about the domain. In such a case, the user may decide not to take the expert system's recommendations (and may note that in an expansion journal so the KE can correct the situation later). However, when the user's decision is an important one, the expert system can still be of some benefit because it can explain what the user can expect to happen if its advice is NOT taken. Making an enlightened decision after deciding to forego the expert system's official recommendation is called intelligent deferral.

"Deferral" refers to the fact that the expert system defers to the user in the final decision. "Intelligent" refers to the fact that the system still offers the user warnings and explanations of what might happen if the system's advice is ignored. In a sense, the system lists the repercussions that could ensue if the system's recommendation is not taken. It is, in effect, saying, "This could happen if you decide not to take my advice, so be careful in these areas."

Intelligent deferral may be built into an expert system in the following circumstances:

- there are many possible answers to a problem (many recommendations the expert system could conceivably make)

- the KE knows that not all the answers have been incorporated into the knowledgebase yet

- the chances of the user not accepting a particular piece of advice are relatively high

- the system is useful to implement even in its current incomplete state

- the user is also the expert (for example, foreign currency trader or telecomm network troubleshooter) using the expert system only as a second set of eyes to catch events that may have slipped by the expert.

- the user needs to know the possible consequences in complex situations

Intelligent deferral can be a way to plug a hole in the expert system. The system can make recommendations on the topics it knows well, but it will defer to the user when a circumstance occurs that its knowledgebase knows nothing about and cannot handle except to give warnings of what might happen if a certain recommendation is not heeded.

Intermediate Conclusions

In a forward chaining expert system, a user may have to wade through a great many questions before the system can present a conclusion and make recommendations. In a backward chaining system, the user may realize that the expert system is asking specific questions to try to prove a certain hypothesis, but the user may have no idea what hypothesis the system is considering. Intermediate conclusions address both those problems by exposing more of the expert system's reasoning, to let the user understand the system's inferences.

Intermediate conclusions allow a user to ask an expert system, at any time in the execution session, what it has concluded so far, based just on what it has been told to that point. It is as if the user were allowed to ask the system, "If this were all the data you had to work with, what would you conclude and recommend?" A backward chaining system then would explain the current hypothesis it is trying to prove. Forward chaining systems would, in a sense, halt execution to draw a conclusion from only the data amassed so far.

A forward chaining system makes intermediate conclusions in one of two ways. One method is to fill in a series of "default" answers (most common or most likely answers) to all the questions the user has left unanswered. In a sense, the system engages in speculation, saying, "Based on what you have told me and what you are likely to tell me, this is my conclusion." Such a system might take the machinery components it has been given, assume that certain cables will be provided, and then configure the machinery, cables and all.

The other method is to mimic a backward chainer and posit a particular hypothesis whenever the user answers a question: one hypothesis for each question. For example, a forward chaining personal financial counseling system might ask about a user's income and, before discovering anything else about the user, infer a high tax bracket from that and temporarily conclude that tax-exempt municipal bonds would

---

be a prime investment consideration. This conclusion can then be put into a file of intermediate conclusions and revealed to the user on demand.

The limitation of intermediate conclusions is that, because they are based on incomplete information, they may be wildly different from a system's final conclusions. However, intermediate conclusions do offer one way of debugging a program: they let an expert look at the conclusions to see if the system is making false assumptions or mistaken hypotheses on its way to a final answer.

Intermediate conclusions provide a window into the thought processes of the expert system, making it less of a black box and more of a rational program. In fact, in some systems, intermediate conclusions are incorporated into a finished system allowing the user, at all times, to have an idea of what the system believes and where its beliefs are leading it.

Implementation Paths

An implementation path is a detailed account of the intended uses of an expert system at each stage in its life cycle. It is not a management plan for *how* the system will be developed, but for *what* the system will do in each of its incarnations along the way to full-scale operation and beyond. An implementation path is a "living document" subject to frequent revision. It establishes the goals, users, and functionality of each phase of expert system implementation. It is a tool often used for long-term project planning. And it describes what will be expected of the expert system at each "freezing" of the system for the users.

Implementation paths were created because expert systems often require years of development before they achieve peak performance. This time frame causes an obvious problem. An expert system that has to be worked on for five years before it can be fielded—with no guarantee that it will be useful when it is finally in place—will be hard to sell to any astute project funder. The need for near-term returns on investment will obviate such a project. Implementation paths ensure that the system is useful early on, while still retaining the ultimate goals of a long-range plan.

Implementation paths aim the system into useful areas that can begin to return investment in the technology before the full system is finished. They allow the system to begin to pay for its own development by being actively employed while it is still under development.

An implementation path may include the following items:

- a list of expected system functionality at each stage in the system's development

- intended users at each stage

- intended uses

- anticipated development times

For example, an expert system created to operate as a commodities market watchdog may be designed to be productive at each level of its development. The system's overall purpose may encompass these goals:

- to monitor indicators presaging imminent international recession or economic resurgence

- to deduce likely effects on cyclical commodities (commodities whose values are sensitive to global economic expansion and contraction, such as aluminum, which often is used less and falls in value during recession because of suppressed consumer demand for automobiles and large appliances)

- to apprise commodities traders of perceived opportunities and dangers

Such a system might require years to become fully operational and useful to traders. But an implementation path would aim the system toward intermediate goals during its development. Each intermediate goal would yield some return on investment for the project funders.

For example, the expert system would *initially* post daily warnings, notices, and graphical market representations. Based on input entered through a keyboard each morning, it would make recommendations to be used by backroom analysts to set the tone for a day's trading.

The same system's *second* incarnation (developed while the first "frozen" version was in operation) would derive input directly from live news and spot rate (price at the moment) feeds. It would post warnings, notices, recommendations, and explanations on a realtime basis to assist the traders in immediate decision making.

The *final* implementation of the same system would also ascertain the composition of individual traders' portfolios and positions, in order to make recommendations specific to each trader's universe and existing positions.

A barebones implementation path for this project, presented by the KE to the project's funders, would be as follows.

- Purposes
    - monitoring inflation/recession/resurgence indicators such as factors that go into the consumer price index composite
    - deducing effects on cyclical commodities
    - apprising managers of trading opportunities/dangers on a daily basis
    - setting the tone for the day's trading
- Users
    - backroom analysts and floor managers
- Input
    - recently announced figures on durable goods orders, personal income, money supply, housing starts, trade balance, cartel agreements, etc., entered through the keyboard each morning by support personnel
- Output
    - "horoscope" for the day's trading; areas of particular caution; areas of perceived opportunity; areas of lackluster performance
- Typical system response
    - "Greater than expected rise in gross national product has occurred.
    - This suggests:
    - Fed may tighten money policy to curb reignition of inflation
    - Consequent rise in interest rates
    - Consequent fall in short-term bonds."
    - "Fall in housing starts has occurred.
    - This suggests:
    - Cyclical commodity to watch: paper/pulp/timber.
    - Recommendation: Caution. Immediate-term fall likely."
- Functionality
    - assesses daily market conditions and makes daily recommendations for action/caution based on a knowledgebase of general meanings of indicators and the influence of indicators on specific cyclicals

---

Second Freezing

- Purposes
  - continuing first freeze recommendations
  - offering projected spot rate movements and recommendations on how to capitalize on them
  - posting warnings, notices, and explanations *in realtime*
- Users
  - individual traders or support personnel assigned to monitor system
- Input
  - livefeeds taken directly from wire services
- Output
  - recommendations for immediate action (system does not execute action itself)
- Typical system response
  - "Expected short-term firming in price of West Texas Intermediate. Background reason: OPEC agreement negotiated for tightening of global supply
  - Immediate reason: Rapid rise in last 6 minutes of WTI price."
- Functionality
  - assesses immediate market conditions and makes immediate recommendations for action based on a knowledgebase of meanings of price movements and the influence of trending/price movements on specific cyclicals

Third Freezing

- Purposes
  - retaining abilities of first and second freezes
  - portfolio maintenance
  - hedging guidance
  - recommendations based on market, individual trader's strategy, current holdings
- Users
  - traders

- Input
  - livefeeds, as in second freeze
  - individual trader's current portfolio
- Output
  - generates trading recommendation, writes order, and awaits confirm/deny/modify signal from trader
- Typical system response
  - "Recommended Purchase: LUMBER 500 MBF at $120/MBF
  - Recommended hedge: 5 CONTRACTS:
  - EACH 120 MBF ON JAN 7
  - (1 MBF = 1000 board feet)"
- Functionality
  - As in second freeze, assesses immediate market conditions and makes immediate recommendations for action based on a knowledgebase of meanings of price movements and the influence of trending/price movements on specific cyclicals; also considers makeup of current portfolio when making recommendations so as to balance the portfolio, spread risk, and devise hedging strategies

This implementation path allows system developers to aim the system at specific goals that will return investment in the project soon, but that will also be in keeping with the project's long-range goals.

An implementation path for such a system guarantees that the system is made useful early on—in its first frozen version—and that it will not have to wait five years before being given to users. Such a system becomes more useful as its development advances.

The final goal for the system's functionality would be the same as for a project that spent five years in secretive development. But the system that followed an implementation path would reach its final implementation via several profit-making steps.

Common Problems 10

The Knowledge Engineer as Thaumaturgist

Most expert systems do not sail to completion without encountering a problem or two. But most difficulties can be resolved within a few days and inflict no permanent damage. The problems mentioned in this chapter, however, may seriously jeopardize an expert system development effort. Some of them will even lead to the demise of a project. But many of them—complex as they are—can be resolved favorably if enough attention is given to their causes.

Lost Status, Diminished Prestige, and Displacement

The successful development of an expert system has as much to do with human ego as machine intelligence; as much to do with political intrigue as technological innovation; as much to do with base instinct as noble intellect or soaring creativity.

Technical problems can make projects difficult. But it is the human, rather than the technical, side of developing expert systems that most often leads to their failure or underachievement. And a KE trying to implement a commercial expert system ignores the odd complexities of human nature at his peril.

An expert system cannot be built against the will of anyone on the development team. And an expert system cannot be foisted on unwilling

138

participants in a project. Consensus building is crucial. Stealth, guile, and subterfuge are no substitute, because ninja knowledge engineering just does not work. Construction of an expert system has to be a cooperative enterprise.

Higher management provides the organizational will to build an expert system. The KE provides the ability and the persistence to get the job done. The domain expert provides the knowledge. And users put the system to work. If the cooperation of any of the individuals involved in the project flags, the system may die of neglect. Even inductive systems which forego the need for an expert (for example, expert systems that review a quantity of historical data and then draw conclusions based on past perceived precedents) still require the cooperation of management, KEs, and users. So ignorance of the motivations of various project participants can be lethal to any development effort.

Enforced Cooperation and Mandatory Volunteers

Domain experts may cooperate in the development of an expert system under duress—for fear of reprimand or under managerial fiat. In such cases, the experts may see the system as an intrusion into their work life. They have an incentive to offer the minimum required time and information to the KE, but nothing beyond that. They may try to assign subordinates to the knowledge acquisition task to keep the knowledge engineer at bay. And they may, in fact, be motivated to denounce the project as valueless in order to get on with their own work.

Similarly, experts who are afraid of being supplanted by an expert system may be motivated to contribute false, incomplete, or misleading information. When such an expert system fails, their jobs will be preserved. So experts may search for subtle ways in which to sabotage the system they are, ostensibly, helping to create.

An expert who derives prestige from a particular job—by being the only one in an organization capable of doing it and being the one person management turns to in a pinch—may shun any system that attenuates that status. That expert's incentive is to prove that the expert system cannot handle the job and to belittle or demean all attempts at reproducing his or her own expert thought processes in a machine.

An Example

The threat of lost prestige, displacement, or reduction in status will undermine any knowledge engineering effort. The classic example of such difficulties is the development of trading/dealing systems.

Bond, commodity, equity, and foreign exchange dealers generate substantial revenues for financial institutions around the world. They also command impressive salaries for their skills.

Traders tend to be single-minded, committed, and impatient with interruptions in their work (especially when they are trading from their own accounts). As a result, they can be painfully uncooperative as domain experts. Part of the reason for cooperation problems with traders may be ignorance on the part of KEs of traders' unique expert system needs:

- the crucial realtime requirements of trading systems

- the lack of space on traders' desks (The hardware device requirement for a project may include the fact that no mouse be used for data input, because the cheese from the pizza that sits on the trader's desk gums up the rotorball of the mouse.)

- the necessarily nanosecond attention spans of dealers

- the fact that an expert system *has to serve* and adapt to the traders, not force them to change their idiosyncratic ways

- the necessity for the system to be non-threatening to its users

Part of the problem is certainly also political. Financial institutions may dearly wish to clone competent traders because of the scarcity of good ones and because of their concentration in certain areas of the world (New York, Tokyo, London). The institutions may have tried "golden handcuffs,"—an attempt to keep traders from jumping to another institution by making their salary or bonuses dependent on the completion of a certain length of stay. And they may have tried to train junior-level people to the level of senior traders—only to see them leave once trained.

Traders, on the other hand, benefit from the dearth of good dealers in the world and, sensibly, are loath to cooperate in any scheme that will make their skills less rare. Trading floor managers in such an environment may see KEs as interfering in their job, which is to manage the generation of revenue and to keep the traders happy, not probe their thought processes. Traders themselves often have no time to offer to someone investigating their success. And upper management will not take kindly to anyone annoying the moneymakers unnecessarily.

All these factors make building deductive expert systems using traders as domain experts a political minefield, one that the KE must cross cautiously and slowly.

Some skills just cannot be cloned into expert systems because of the reluctance of experts. (Traders, for example, still have never been entirely cloned, though they have been supported in their work by expert systems.)

The KE's job in such an environment is to ascertain whether an expert system is possible, considering the political environment, and whether a way can be found to ensure that *all* project participants benefit from the system's creation. Managers should be able to see a return on their investment, rather than a reduction in their headcount or profitability. Users should see less work for themselves or a rise in their prestige because they become the purveyors of expert information. Experts should see themselves as being freed from mundane problems and allowed to tackle more sophisticated conundrums (in the case of traders, being allowed to make more money by letting the expert system handle more routine matters). And no one should see his or her own status or importance to an organization decline because of the expert system's construction.

Another Example

DP/MIS departments are responsible for maintaining the beating heart of all large organizations. They generate payrolls, critical information for high-level decision making, and reports on every aspect of a company's financial and bureaucratic life. They always have more work than they can handle—backlogs of user requests stretching back a year or more are not uncommon. In such a frenetic environment, new technology may languish untested and unused because it represents a time demand in a time-short department. Trying to prod expert system development in such an organization may meet with considerable resistance from MIS managers who already have a full schedule and find it difficult to assign people to engage in expert system development work with so many pressing and immediate needs around them.

Often the solution to the problem of dealing with "immediate needs only" departments is to operate outside their boundaries. A skunkworks (a semiautonomous group dedicated to development work) may be the answer. But the politics of establishing such a group has to be considered. A group that sees itself as an outlaw band free to thumb its nose at the MIS department will cause more problems than it solves. And a group of "pure scientists" free to diddle and tweak, with no deadlines or quantifiable objectives, may accomplish little of value to an organization. So the charter of every skunkworks should include specific deliverables.

Choosing a Tool First

The only serious mistake a tool selector can make—a mistake from which there may be no recovery—is to choose a tool *before* understanding the expert system application to be tackled. Every tool has its strengths and its limitations. No tool does *everything* well (despite vendors' claims). And to saddle KEs with, say, a backward chaining diagnostic-specific tool that genuinely hampers development of their forward chaining scheduling/planning system may condemn a project to failure at the start.

A manufacturing application, for example, that requires the frame-based representation of knowledge (as in the subassemblies of parts for a large piece of equipment) may need an object- or frame-based expert system development tool. Similarly, an analytic application for trouble-shooting telecommunications equipment malfunctions may require the system's ability to assume problem causes and to backward chain to test them. Different tools might be required for each of these problems.

A KE will have to abide by a tool's constraints once the tool has been purchased, so it is always best to study possible expert system applications before selecting a tool. This is not as much of a problem as it once was, since most development tools seem to be growing more similar to each other with each revision. But it still behooves a buyer to beware and to make certain the tool handles what will be required of it in a given application.

Underestimating Integration and Hybridization

Integration is the task of tying expert systems to conventional systems. Hybridization is the task of building conventional programming abilities into an expert system. Both tasks can be formidable endeavors. And neither can be blithely dismissed if an expert system is ever to be actually used (not just tested) by an organization.

Very few expert systems are useful as standalones. Most organizations require the expert system to work in an environment with conventional systems and databases. So hybridization and integration are, practically speaking, inevitable in the development of commercial expert systems beyond the toy or touchstone (feasibility tester) level. Integration is a problem that cannot be ignored if useful expert systems are ever to be built in any organization.

With that in mind, some of the usual difficulties of integration and their solutions should be considered before a project is well underway.

Hardware Integration

If an expert system is to run on one type of hardware and conventional programs on another, the physical linking of machinery is the first integration hurdle to be leapt. In some cases, even the linkage of different models sold by the same manufacturer may be impossible (data communication protocols may forbid interconnection). But in some cases, the interconnection of hardwares from different manufacturers is a simple matter.

Obviously, it is crucial to discover any physical linkage limitations *before* time and resources are dedicated to expert system development. An expert system that can exist only in a data communications vacuum is likely to be of no use to anyone except as an interesting research project. So hardware connectability is important to discover in the early stages of a project.

Software Integration

If an expert system is to reside on the same physical hardware (same disk) or the same logical hardware (same cluster or network) as the conventional system with which it will interact, then the linkage of hardwares will not be a problem.

But integrating softwares can be a far more onerous and time-consuming task than physically linking machines. (This is, of course, a central problem in human interaction as well. It requires less than a day to fly to Tokyo from any international airport in the world—a hardware problem. However, understanding enough of the language and culture to conduct business there—software integration—may take years.) And software integration often becomes the most critical problem to be resolved in a project especially when the expert system is large, complex, and highly integrated.

Differing operating systems, differing high-level programming languages, differing database models, and differing program needs (for example, data vs. knowledge) all contribute to the babel of software integration. The following "rules" will help a KE sort through and resolve this confusion.

Begin with the Prototype Itself, not the Software Linkages

Software integration for a large system sometimes requires *more* time and effort than the development of the expert system itself. So, it is easy to sink into the muck and mire of integration problems and not emerge for months; meanwhile the expert system languishes.

To circumvent this problem, begin with the expert system rather than the integration work. Once it is certain that software links between an expert system and the conventional world are possible, determine the format in which data will enter the expert system. Begin by building the prototype using dummy input in that format. Do not begin by making software links between conventional systems and the expert system unless the expert system is small and will remain so in future.

If one KE is building an entire large system, start with the expert system and make the linkages later. If there are several engineers on a project, tasks can be done in parallel. But let the linkage work be subservient to the expert system development work.

Realize That Change Is Inevitable

Be careful of committing to one format of integration early on and forcing the expert system to be rewritten around it. The expert system may change significantly during the course of its development, and input from conventional systems that might have seemed crucial in the beginning may prove useless at the end. So start by assessing the expert system's needs, rather than the requirements of linkage.

Building a prototype is as much a process of discovery as of construction. And unanticipated discoveries about what the expert system really requires in the way of input may obviate the need for much of someone's hard work in integrating softwares. Initial time is better spent on the expert system than on the links. Once the input needs of the expert system have been solidified, the integration work can begin.

Small, Time-Critical Expert Systems May Have to Be Directly Linked to Conventional Systems

Direct linkage involves passing data directly from, say, a FORTRAN program to an OPS5 program. *Indirect* linkage means passing data from the FORTRAN program to a flat file or a database and then allowing the OPS5 program to retrieve the data from the file (blackboard) whenever it finds a need for it.

If the expert system is small, has meager integration needs, and its execution speed is a critical issue, then directly linking expert and conventional systems together may be justified. Such directly linked systems may include those that handle time-critical activities. An expert system providing immediate on-line air traffic control recommendations based on livefeed radar data, for example, may require direct links between expert system and radar. Instantaneous telecommunications network routing expert systems, which switch phone calls between trunks and exchanges on a realtime basis to free up overused lines, may need direct links. And airline reservation monitoring projects that use an expert system to monitor the performance of several mainframes processing reservation data will require direct links in order to act quickly when they recognize "CPU binding" (overworked reservation-handling machines whose workload must be redirected to other machines).

In each of these cases, the number of linkages to conventional systems may be as few as one, and performance requirements necessitate the shortest possible input/output time between systems. Direct linkage in such an environment makes the most sense.

But not all expert systems should be directly linked to conventional systems. External blackboards should be used when the system is large and complex or when expert systems will share data with each other or with more than one other conventional program.

If the expert system is large and complex and the linkages are many, then indirect linkage to conventional systems is more likely to yield an understandable, maintainable system. Indirect linkage is done through the use of external blackboards ("external" meaning that the blackboard is outside any one program and is used by more than one program). A conventional program may write relevant data onto the blackboard, and an expert system may retrieve those data to use in inferencing.

Indirect linkages allow the complex web of data interdependencies to be reduced to a single locus of activity. An expert system need only communicate with the blackboard, using the blackboard's format for data. And each conventional system or database need only deal with the blackboard rather than with each other and the expert system. This is especially helpful for future maintainers of the system when a project involves passing data from several different languages or database formats into the expert system. Programmers working specifically on improving the expert system need not understand both the expert system language *and* the particular conventional language to extract data from the blackboard. They need understand only what the data will look like when they are placed in the blackboard by the conventional programs.

Indirect linkages often increase the speed at which a large expert system runs. Directly linked systems are often daemon driven. (A daemon is a rule that fires opportunistically when certain factors appear, regardless of the program's usual planned agenda of operations.) The directly linked expert system waits for data from the conventional system and acts as soon as the new data come in. Indirectly linked systems, on the other hand, allow the expert system and the conventional systems to act in their own time.

Too Broad, Too Diffuse, Too Complex, or Too Arcane a Problem

Unbounded Domain

An *unbounded domain* is a problem that usually reveals itself early on in a project's development. It implies that a particular task requires too much knowledge in too many areas to be able to fit neatly into an expert system. An application may, during prospecting, appear to be manageable. But when the system is actually put through its first paces during early prototyping, the amount of knowledge the expert uses to make decisions is found to be much greater than anticipated, and the unbounded domain reveals itself.

For example, if an organization wants an expert system to do commodity price forecasting, such a system may begin by examining only financial data such as spot rates and contracts outstanding, a well-bounded domain. But a drought occurring in Brazil will suddenly influence the price of Costa Rican coffee. So a useful predictive expert system will require some meteorological knowledge to consider the effect of global weather patterns on commodity prices.

The signing of a trade agreement between the Americans and the Caribbean nations will instantly affect the price of sugar in Australia. Thus, a useful commodity price forecasting expert system should also consider political and diplomatic factors in its decision making.

And a nuclear accident in Chernobyl, Soviet Georgia, the country's principal grain-growing region, will result in higher Argentine and

Canadian wheat prices. So the expert system may even require some knowledge of technological dangers in order to assess commodities adequately.

The need for some understanding on the part of the expert system in all of these areas may not be obvious at the start, but it may eventually kill a project whose goal was to be thorough enough to replace human experts.

Unbounded domains can be discovered and avoided before a system is prototyped if the expert is asked to reveal early on all the pieces of data used in decision making. A list of every data source and some time spent watching the expert at work can help to confirm that a knowledgebase can, in fact, be built to do the expert's task, without the system needing "common sense" or encyclopedic knowledge.

Subjective Criteria

Subjective criteria are strategies used by an expert in decision making that cannot easily be encoded into an expert system. For example, when a manufacturing engineer diagnosing an equipment problem says he knows there is a problem with the turbines because they "sound funny," that expert is using a subjective criterion. When a welder says the oxyacetylene torch flame must be "very blue," or a paper maker says more titanium must be added to the slurry because the paper is "too dark," those experts are using subjective criteria.

In some cases, statistical or fuzzy logic techniques can be used to imitate, inside the expert system, the expert's perceptions. "Too dark" paper can be quantified and a meter designed to detect the paper's albedo (reflectivity of light), or a chart with colors and adjectives ("This color is what too dark looks like. This is just right. This is too light.") can be distributed to users of the expert system so they can answer the diagnostic question, "Is the paper too dark?"

But in many cases, the criteria used by the expert just cannot be encoded. "Sounds funny," "Something tells me," and "Feels wrong" are all phrases that signal criteria that because of their subjectivity may not be able to be entered into an expert system.

The names and domain details have been changed in these cases, but the problems and solutions described are exactly as they occurred.

Case 1: Organizational Failure

The senior vice president (VP) of a large American manufacturing firm considers the construction of an expert system to assist with, and eventually take over, the task of shop floor planning at the company's newest manufacturing facility in the Pacific Northwest. He contacts the New Technologies group within his company and assigns the manager of the group the task of implementing the new system.

At the same time, the chief operations officer (COO) of a U.S.-based multinational financial services corporation sets out to institute development of a series of expert systems to assist company Customer Service representatives in all regions of the U.S., with an eye toward extending the systems to offices in Europe and Japan in two years' time. She contacts the Advanced Systems department because they have a strong reputation within the company as expert system developers. She assigns the job to the group and follows up on their progress.

After six months, the manufacturing VP asks the New Tech group to give a short presentation on their automation of shop floor planning and to present their results, preferably in the form of a working prototype. In the same week, the financial services COO contacts the Advanced Systems department head and requests a demonstration or slide presentation describing the Customer Service expert system. Both managers appear at the information-exchange meetings hoping to see palpable results. But both are disappointed.

The financial services COO sees a full-color slide show on "what the system will look like," but no code. Dozens of complex organizational spiderweb charts are presented detailing how each group in the company will be affected by the system when it is built. But no system is shown. When a computer is wheeled in, the COO's hopes are buoyed. But the computer screen is used only to display a moving 3-D graphical diagram of how information will flow within the organization when the system is made operational. And a 12-page handout is offered that lists all the university degrees that the group members hold along with the technical papers each has authored.

Being fully aware of what is involved in expert system development, the COO begins to probe for direct answers. "Who has been identified as the expert in the Customer Service department? When will the first prototype be shown to the experts? When to the users? How will the system be integrated into the Customer Service databases? Who will maintain the system after full implementation?" No useful answers are forthcoming. She decides to investigate further after the meeting.

On the same afternoon, the manufacturing VP is being dolefully enlightened. The New Tech group manager begins the meeting by listing the educational credentials of each group member. He then launches into an involved disquisition on the nature of complex search strategies in large expert system networks and ends by enumerating the expert systems currently being designed in AI labs around the world, emphasizing how important expert systems will be for the future of the company.

The VP is stunned. Not a single word was spoken about the shop floor expert system putatively under development. He asks if, perhaps, what he has just heard are prefatory remarks, with a demonstration of the prototype to follow. But there is no system to show. The meeting ends with the VP—who himself is under the gun to get this system developed—visibly angry.

Both managers dig into the history and past accomplishments of the groups assigned to build the systems. Each delivers an ultimatum to the group to come up with results in six months.

Resources are not the problem. Each group is swimming in expensive hardware and software. The COO discovers that the section of the building that houses the Advanced Systems group is known in company vernacular as "the sandbox." The VP notices a hand-drawn sign that says "The Electronic Playpen" taped to the door of a New Tech office. The COO discovers that the past expert systems ostensibly developed by the Advanced Systems group were, in fact, chiefly built by hired consultants. The VP finds that the New Tech organization has swelled to over 100 employees, but when presented with a list of the group's past and current projects, he cannot find a single project that has been delivered to another group.

At the end of the second six months, two of the Advanced Systems group's 12 members have left the company. The manager of the group then explains to the COO that the expert system could not be built on time because of insufficient personnel (only 10 people). At the same time, the manufacturing VP also finds that the floor planning expert system has not been built, but "too much other work for the [100] people in the group" is the stated reason. Both expert system development projects are judged to be complete failures. Both projects have yielded no results.

What both managers come to realize is that several factors have conspired to make their advanced technology groups ineffective:

- The groups hire people on the basis of academic credentials, rather than on the basis of direct experience in commercial expert system construction. People in the group are measured against inappropriate (non-business) criteria. This problem is compounded by the fact that once groups develop a critical mass of people they become self-policing. As a result, after a while, the group makes a conscious effort to hire only people with similar backgrounds and interests, which include researching and designing but not actually delivering expert systems. The group forgets that it operates within the bounds of a business and begins to measure itself along the lines of a university (Ph.D.s per capita) rather than a business (profits per capita).

- The groups have been allowed the luxury of designing expert systems without having to implement them profitably. They have become, essentially, advisers to the people who would build the systems, rather than the builders themselves. This leads to big promises and incommensurate results.

- The groups are sheltered from profit/loss review. They are looked at as Research and Development (R&D) overhead, rather than as direct contributors to the corporations' revenues. The groups are not held accountable for the money they spend, so they become sinkholes of money and technical talent.

- The groups become isolated from reality in the well-meaning attempt to shield them from burdensome daily operational concerns. Both groups were originally intended as skunkworks— semiautonomous organizations free to roam around solving problems without managerial interference. But the groups quickly devolved into ones without any kind of managerial oversight. In time, they became entirely self-serving, uninterested, and unaffected by the concerns of the company at large and intent only on impressing each other with diplomas.

- The charter of the groups is inappropriate. The groups were initially created *"to maintain the in-house capability to build advanced systems"* when they should have been created *"to actually build advanced systems."* There is even a certain amount of prestige involved in having researchers well known in the AI field working for the company in the advanced tech groups, regardless of the groups' failure to deliver systems. Prestige and degrees overrule business concerns.

Both the VP and the COO discover that there are three ways in which expert systems are developed in a company. Systems are built *from the top down* when a high-level manager initiates a development project. Systems are built *from the bottom up* when a programmer takes the initiative to learn the technology and begins stealing time away from other pursuits to build an expert system to show to management. And systems are developed (but not implemented) *round-and-round* within the confines of a group set up to do nothing but experiment with technology: drawing up plans for systems, refining the plans, giving seminars on the plans, and then drawing up new improved plans.

Solution

To set the situation to rights, both managers enact two changes. First, they go directly to the organizations in which the expert systems will reside (the shop floor and the Customer Service department) and find, to their considerable surprise, that expert system work is already underway on a small scale in both organizations. The new projects are then assigned directly to those groups, and functioning prototypes are demonstrated six weeks later in both groups, with no assistance from the advanced technology departments.

Secondly, they reevaluate the New Tech and Advanced Systems group charters. The manufacturing New Tech group (100 people) is entirely disbanded, and its members are given the chance to find jobs within the company in the next several months or face dismissal. The financial services Advanced Systems group (10 people) becomes the semiautonomous group it was meant to be and is assigned to do "contract work" for other groups within the company. It is made subject to quarterly reviews which decide whether the group can justify its hardware, software, and personnel costs based on its revenue generation for other groups in the company. (After three years under this new system, the group still exists and, in fact, is flourishing, but it has retained none of its original members.)

Both the Shop Floor Planner and the Customer Service Assistant expert systems are fully implemented within the year.

A software engineer (a COBOL programmer writing payroll programs) in a government agency's MIS organization decides to stay late in the evenings and come in on weekends to build an expert system using the LISP language that was included free with a group of software packages recently installed on the agency's workstation network. He teaches himself the language and then gathers information from an expert in the Cash Management department during lunch hours and breaks, gradually amassing a set of rules to be used in taking over the cash budgeting task. He includes rules on the types of investments made by the agency, their maturities, their interest rates, the banks and broker-age houses the investments are made through, and the times of regular disbursements and distributions made by the agency.

After several months of effort, the engineer shows the embryonic system to the cash management expert. He then incorporates the expert's initial feedback into the program's functionality. In another month, the system actually begins to make rational cash management decisions. And the cash management expert begins to recognize the new program's potential. However, having been well trained by the MIS group to get all requests for program enhancement right the first time ("That change will take ten weeks and cost you $10,000"), the expert is hesistant to suggest any changes in the code once he sees the program working. With encouragement from the KE, however, he asks for some revisions, is shown the changes enacted in code the very next day, and eventually begins to get comfortable with the rapid modifications which are part of the prototyping process.

During this time, the cash manager begins to talk about the system at weekly meetings with his boss. Word travels, and the KE is sum-moned to the corner office along with his MIS manager to discuss the new R&D effort. The project receives official approval, and the KE is taken off other work to concentrate on the expert system project. A demonstration is arranged for four weeks hence, enough time for the KE to make the linkage from the expert system to the cash management databases.

Unfortunately, the MIS manager is livid because he was not informed of this project earlier. When he is told that the project was being done on off-hours, he replies it was also being done on company hardware, so he should have been notified. And he is angry that a capable programmer has been taken off payroll programming—when his group is already shorthanded—just to toy with a blue-sky academic research project.

During the next week, the KE, who spends every evening pouring over manuals, makes the links between the databases and the expert system. This is lucky because the demo date is moved up three weeks at the request of the MIS manager, who has recently informed his boss: "We tried AI two years ago and it didn't work. There's no reason to think it'll work now."

The KE scrambles to get the database links solidly in place and to clean up the user interface. But one hour before the demo, the database is brought down by the MIS group "for an emergency reorganization." The KE quickly reverts to an older version of his program that pulls data from a dummy database created for testing purposes.

During the demo, the MIS manager is noticeably surprised to see data streaming in from somewhere. He asks to sit at the keyboard himself to do the demo, to show "how a new user would work the system." He answers a few questions on disbursement dates and then quickly types in a nonsensical response and hits the return key while asking, "What if we just said this?" The system comes back with "Please retype. Did not understand response."—a part of the user interface put in by the KE. The manager's face reddens.

After several requests for data from the user and several dips into the dummy database, the expert system rolls out a comprehensive listing of recommended investments and their redemption dates. Even the MIS manager is impressed, albeit begrudgingly so.

However, at the meeting with the agency head to discuss continuance of the project, the MIS director makes the following negative points:

- The expert system is written in LISP, a language none of the other programmers knows. If the system is implemented and the developer leaves, who will maintain it?

- There is no telling how long it will take to finish construction of the expert system because the prototyping process is open-ended. It could lead anywhere and incorporate any of the cash manager's functions.

- A COBOL programmer cannot be spared from the group when the MIS department has such a large backlog of work.

After considering all the points made, the agency head assigns the KE to work on payroll programs half time and on expert system development half time. The MIS manager, however, assigns a large load of payroll programming to the KE, who is then forced to do the expert system development work nights and weekends again. Eventually, the programmer leaves the agency, takes a job elsewhere as a fulltime KE, and builds a cash management expert system, followed by a foreign exchange system, followed by a bond trading system....

Case 3: Failure Due to Ego

A newly formed Artificial Intelligence group in a multinational telecommunications firm assigns one of its members to construct an expert system for realtime network failure analysis.

The expert working with the KE travels all over the world deducing the causes of network snags, slowdowns, and crashes at regional American, European, and Asian sites. He is the only person the company trusts in the job, and he is highly paid for his knowledge. The expert has trained people who have come to him from other sites (usually after a substantial problem at that site), so he is accustomed to discussing his thought processes and methods of diagnosis. Most of his time in the last several years has been spent consulting on problems in the regional sites.

The expert is about 40 years old, unmarried, known to be very ambitious for his career, and nowhere close to retirement.

The knowledge acquisition process begins well. The expert appears to be flattered by the presence of yet another student sent by the head office to sit at the feet of the master. The KE asks about the expert's duties, and the expert is open and willing to assist, so the first few interviews go smoothly. The KE discovers that the mental diagnostic processes employed by the expert are extraordinarily complex. And the KE is genuinely impressed with the expert's depth and breadth of practical problem-solving knowledge.

The project looks as if it is on the road to success. However, the acquisition process grinds to a halt soon after the first prototype demonstration to the expert. The problem is that the expert sees for the first time what the computer program is meant to do—emulate his own thought processes—and becomes pensive and reticent. He asks, "What will this system eventually be able to do?" The KE explains what he had mentioned in the first meeting: that the system will clone the expert. The expert then apparently realizes what will happen to his own high-prestige, high-pay job when a computer program diagnoses network flaws as well as he does. He suddenly remembers an appointment in another city.

The next day, the KE finds that the next four scheduled knowledge acquisition meetings— all the meetings for the next month—have been canceled. The expert has left for Europe.

The KE proceeds as best he can for two months, trying to incorporate into the expert system some of the relevant heuristics gleaned from company manuals written by the expert. But in time he runs out of knowledge to encode.

The expert is nowhere to be seen. He extends his trip to Europe, then departs for Singapore. He has conferences to attend and fires to put out at regional sites in Asia. He requests and is granted a reassignment to the U.S. west coast. The KE, however, remains on the east coast.

The project dies. The head office sends an official memo exhorting the expert to resume the construction of the expert system. But the memo is carefully worded so as not to offend or threaten an expert whose skills are so rare and necessary to the health of the company. The expert finds far too many emergencies to attend to to participate in the design of the expert system. The KE spends his time making links between the expert system and the realtime network monitoring systems, but after a year has passed, the KE requests reassignment to another project.

Solution

The KE is called to participate in a post-mortem meeting on the failed network advisor expert system. He suggests that the reason the expert was initially cooperative was that he did not realize the capabilities of an expert system. The KE says the expert may have felt threatened by the system when he did understand it, because it would obviously eliminate the need for a globe-roaming network troubleshooter. Building the expert system would essentially result in the expert's demotion from highly respected expert to occasional advisor. Since the expert was not about to retire, he had no incentive to cooperate in the removal of his only job.

When the KE is asked for a suggestion, he says that the expert "needs a reason to cooperate." He suggests that the expert be "offered a promotion or bonus *contingent on his building an expert system to take over the troubleshooting task.*" No expert system to replace the expert would mean no promotion for the expert. That should motivate the expert to encourage development of the expert system. It will also make the company less of a hostage to the expert's abilities: once the expert system is in place, the expert can leave and not cripple the company's ability to handle network emergencies.

The meeting ends without a decision being made. But a week later the expert himself calls the KE and explains that he has allocated several weeks to work on nothing but the expert system (and that he has moved his office back to the east coast). Obviously, the expert has been offered the promotion if the system is built.

The problem then becomes restraining the expert's urge to declare the system finished. The expert now has strong motivation to see the system done, so he can assume his new position. The KE, the expert's manager, and the users who will adopt the completed expert system become the restraining forces of the project, keeping the expert honest.

In the end, the system is finished and fielded, the expert promoted, and the expert system made operational in all regional offices.

Demonstrating an Expert System   11

The Knowledge Engineer as Marketer

At certain points in its life cycle, every expert system will have to be
demonstrated. In fact, the iterative nature of the prototyping process
guarantees that an expert system will be shown more than once to
domain experts, users, managers, and project funders.

Giving the demo involves more than just tapping keyboard buttons
and repeating, "When we do this, this happens." It means distilling and
codifying knowledge that may have taken the KE months to acquire
and presenting that knowledge in a format suitable to the audience's
abilities and interests.

Ideally, the KE's goal is to build a system that eventually will be
demonstrated to management by the system's *users,* not the system's
developers. The KE has an obvious interest in the system's success, since
it represents his or her own skill and ability. But users are more likely
to be impartial (and believable) to a project funder because they must
be confident enough in the expert system's benefits to agree to give the
demo. And having users convey enthusiasm for a system sits better with
project funders than developers expressing their natural endorsement
for the system.

Regardless of who the demonstrater is, however, all expert system
presenters generally discover that giving a demo successfully becomes
a matter of distancing oneself from one's own experience with the
expert system and seeing the demo through the eyes of a beginner. No

matter how many times the demo has been given, the presenter has to remember that the audience may never have seen the system before. This means that explanations must be forthcoming for every feature that is likely to puzzle the audience. And those explanations must be concise, precise, and lucid.

Before Demonstrating

Before actually demonstrating the system, the KE should keep a few "rules" in mind.

Do Not Condescend or Baffle

What is most important in presenting a demo is that the audience's understanding increase during the demo presentation. Smoke and mirrors, fast talk, conjuring tricks, or purposefully confusing patter will all be transparent to an audience, if not immediately, then later, on reflection. Such practices can do nothing but jeopardize a presenter's credibility.

Each demo should be tailored to the knowledge level of the audience, so the presenter does not condescend to a domain-sophisticated group or perplex a domain-innocent group.

The audience should learn something from the demo about the benefits of the expert system, its place in their world, and its extrapolation to other problems they may be facing.

Draw on What the Audience Knows

A system that diagnoses "warping problems in the manufacture of corrugatorboard" may seem pretty remote from the experience of most people. In such a case, a KE might begin by explaining that corrugatorboard is used to make the boxes most of us carry possessions in when moving to a new residence. The KE might also explain that the three layers of corrugatorboard—an inner and outer liner and a corrugated medium in between—can be seen when a box is torn across the grain. In this way, corrugatorboard manufacture becomes a concrete problem to solve, rather than an abstraction.

Know What Kind of Information
the Audience Needs

Make an effort to understand the perspective of the audience. A group of managers may want only an overview of technical matters, but considerable detail as to how the expert system will influence their organization (for example, increase productivity or accuracy, system development time, or necessary tools). A technical audience, on the other hand, may demand excruciating detail on knowledge representation or inferencing mechanisms, but want only a summary of returns on investment.

A KE can do considerable harm by trying to forcefeed technical information to a managerial audience or substituting marketing fluff for program specifications with a technical group. It is best to discover ahead of time the group's interests and to address those interests directly.

Pay Attention to User Interface

After spending eight months resolving a grueling knowledge representation conundrum in an expert system, a KE may demonstrate the program to users only to hear them all ooh and ah over the eight colors the monitor can display. This may be disconcerting to any KE who takes pride in his or her technical ability, but it is inevitable when giving demos. Colors are impressive. Movement is impressive. Icons are impressive. Regardless of the sophistication of the inferencing or the inheritance, the user interface is the only part of the system that the users ever see. So it has to be attended to. Human factors have to be considered.

Font size, for example, should always be as large as practically possible when an expert system is being demonstrated. Color often conveys meaning that would not be available in any other way. And users usually apprehend graphics sooner and more easily than text.

Work from the General to the Particular

Intricate details need a foundation. Address specific technical, project management, and business considerations only after the audience understands the general aim and purpose of the expert system.

Place the Expert System in a Domain Context

The expert system should be placed in the context of the industry whose problems it addresses, to keep it from looking like a disembodied academic project.

For example, an expert system that recommends solutions to long-distance digital transmission telephony problems solves a small difficulty in the larger realm of telecommunications. Such an expert system can be used by 1) help desk operators stationed at customer service phones, 2) field personnel to answer customer questions without having to call headquarters, or 3) large customers directly. Such an explanation roots the expert system in the domain in which it does service. The expert system then becomes "a telecommunications problem solver," rather than just an ethereal "AI project."

Explain Why the Expert System Was Built

Expert systems are built for particular reasons. Elucidating those reasons can help an audience understand both the application itself and the forces that prod the development of expert systems in general.

The evaluation of hypothecated real estate (property used as collateral for a loan), for example, can be a difficult problem for Japanese financial services companies, because of factors unique to the Japanese marketplace. The amount of sunlight received by a building, traffic patterns surrounding the property, and disguised ownership of the building all influence its resale value. Because Japanese management often encourages generalization among employees, jobs often are rotated every few years. As a result, expertise in real estate evaluation can be accumulated, then lost, on a regular basis. Both the non-formulaic nature of the task in this case and the organization's high in-house turnover rate suggest the development of an expert system for this domain.

Offer a Scenario for a Specific Problem

For example, the presenter may explain, "For purposes of this demonstration, let us say that I am the foreign exchange manager of a multinational computer manufacturer whose headquarters are in the U.S. We have a wholly owned subsidiary in Japan which is buying integrated circuits for us in Malaysia. We intend to sign a contract for the circuits this week, but payment will not be made in Malaysian currency by the Japanese subsidiary for six months.

"In the next six months, the value of the Malaysian ringgit may rise in relation to the Japanese yen. Or the yen may rise in relation to the U.S. dollar. We may find ourselves paying out more in actual dollars than we had intended when we negotiated the deal. This presents us with a hedging problem.

"Hedging is the protection of profits from fluctuations in exchange rates over time. In this case, we have three currencies to consider in the protection of our profits. The expert system will assist us in this hedging task."

In this way, the expert system has been given a specific problem to solve during the demonstration. The KE is not just "out walking the dog," but is solving a real-world problem in front of the audience.

Detail How the System Solves the Problem

An explanation of how the expert system solves a problem may help an audience visualize the system's use in other areas. Or it may help the audience identify potential shortcomings of the expert system while there is still time to address such problems. So let an audience know how the system thinks, what data it studies to reach a conclusion, and what it assumes about the world before making decisions.

For example, a presenter may be showing a securities analysis (stock valuation) inductive system to equity trading support people (those involved in analyzing the stock market to assist in large-scale stock purchases/sales and hedging).

The demonstrator may say, "This expert system is familiar with 7000 past cases of sudden market fluctuation from the October 1929 crash to the most recent significant correction. It looks at current market conditions and compares those conditions to its case histories of rapid drops and rises in the market. It then predicts the chances of sudden volatility in the current market.

"When it recognizes a salient pattern of market activity, the system announces its findings, gives its reasoning, and then identifies potential broad-based index option buy/sell opportunities." (An index option is a way of simply buying or selling the entire stock market or large pieces of it, rather than a basket of hundreds of individual stocks.)

Such an explanation removes the mysticism of AI. It reveals the system's "thought processes" and will often allow first-time viewers of the system to make constructive suggestions on system development after only a single demo.

Explain Why an Expert System Was Needed

Detail why an expert system is the proper choice for problem solution and why a conventional approach would not work as well or at all. Explain why it was necessary to turn to an expert system to solve the problem.

(Handouts of the slides may also be appropriate.) The slides may include the following contents:

- a picture of the type of equipment used in the domain the expert system deals with or of the process involved (for example, how corrugatorboard is manufactured or what a telecommunications switching network looks like)

- an illustration of the specific problem (for example, a picture of warped corrugatorboard or of a complex network)

- an explanation of the intent of the expert system (for example, realtime process control or anomaly detection)

- an explanation of where the AI is in the solution of the problem (for example, a non-numeric, non-monotonic system that offers explanations, infers, makes decisions, and assists in its own expansion)

- a list of the intended users of the system

- a list of possible extrapolations of the expert system (for example, a similar system may be used in the detection of computer network security risks or in the manufacture of quality grade bleached paper)

- a graphical representation of any links to databases, livefeeds, sensors, conventional programs, blackboards, or other expert systems

Explain All Terms and Concepts

It is usually best to assume that the audience will be unfamiliar with expert system concepts. If it is a mixed group (managers, MIS staff, potential users), some members may even be unfamiliar with the particular industry problem being treated.

So, have *brief* (one-sentence) explanations at hand for all technical (not just AI) concepts and a clear illustrative example for each. Volunteer the explanations as soon as the concept is mentioned.

Briefly Explain What Tools, Languages,
Hardware Configurations, etc., Were Used
in the System's Construction

Some audience members may be charged with developing or implementing expert systems in their organizations and will be especially interested in the tools necessary to do so. Other, non-technical members, may at least want to know the names of the tools involved for future reference.

The Demo Itself

While viewing the opening/introductory screen, offer a scenario under which the expert system would be used.

A KE may want to explain the following:

- who would use the system

- why someone would use it

- in what type of organizational setting it would be used

- under what circumstances it would be used

Point to Something of Interest on Each Screen

Features to be pointed out along the way may include a method of dealing with information unique to AI, a feature of the system of particular value to its users, or an ability of the expert system not found in any conventional system.

Read Text off the Screen or Summarize Large
Blocks of Text When They Appear on the Screen

Remember that, while a demonstrator may have read the text a hundred times, the user may never have seen it before. Reading the screen aloud while the audience is looking at it will reinforce the message of the screen. And summarizing reams of text on the screen will allow the audience to understand its content without having to slog through it. But speaking on another topic while the audience is trying to read will result in confusion for the audience. So it's best to deal with the text that appears on the screen.

Know the Demo Well Enough to be Flexible
in Responses to the Audience

If a certain feature seems to be of particular interest, expand on the use of that feature in the system. The following features may be worth explaining:

- explanation facilities
- intelligent deferral
- expansion logs or journals
- graphical responses or explanations

Be Truthful and Open

Human beings have an uncanny knack for recognizing fraud, no matter how cleverly disguised. This fact is sometimes the demo presenter's incentive to understand the demo's domain and functionality thoroughly.

Rehearse Alone First, Then in Front
of a Friendly Audience

Accept questions eagerly. The more questions colleagues ask, the better prepared a demo presenter will be in future. Take special note of questions that are asked frequently. Proper preparation during rehearsals may keep the air from becoming dark with vegetables during the actual demo presentation.

Appendixes

A Case Study   *A*

The Knowledge Engineer as Generalist

The following case study is a condensed composite of five actual cases of expert system development. The names and details of the domain have been changed. But the conversations and reports are close to verbatim. And the process of developing the expert system through its various stages is recorded just as it happened in the five original cases.

Throughout this case study, the thoughts of the knowledge engineer are printed in italics.

Case Background

We are at the headquarters of PolyBak Inc., a company that produces natural resin film and paper packaging products. The company has a reputation for being forward thinking and environmentally benign in its application of technology. And the company is proud of its non-polluting manufacturing facilities and practices. It also sees itself as a leader in the packaging field.

PolyBak has seven main in-house divisions: Paper and Resin Production, Packaging Manufacture, Sales and Marketing, Waste Treatment, Shipping/Distribution, MIS, and Treasury. Any one of these divisions may eventually house an expert system.

Paper and resin production are handled in nine plants scattered throughout the U.S. The package manufacturing plants, to which uncut paper and resin are shipped by rail, are in the same nine states. Wastewater is treated at all plants in a series of outdoor glass cylinders filled with living organisms that break down the waste and convert it into harmless elements. Overland shipping between the plants is handled by rail and by a fleet of retrofitted hydrogen-powered trucks for shipment to large retail customers and wholesalers. Overseas shipping is negotiated with outside maritime shipping companies. The MIS department keeps the books and records. And the Treasury department for this multinational corporation manages cash, debt, currencies, and investments.

Our Research on the Company

PolyBak creates two types of packaging: paper/cellulose and a natural plastic-like resin made from casein (milk protein). The opaque resin film can be used to wrap consumer products for up to one year if it is not allowed to contact the soil. It will be entirely digested by soil microbes in seven days when placed in contact with bare moist earth, leaving no harmful residue behind. The film currently is being used to package popcorn and candies. No chlorine bleaching agents are used on the paper or resin—oxygen bleaching only. And soy-based inks are used for coloring instead of titanium-, lead-, or mercury-based tinting agents.

The factories that produce the finished packaging materials from the uncut paper and resin run on a 24-hour, 7-day-a-week basis as long as there are orders to fill. A scheduler is assigned to each paper/resin plant and to each package manufacturing plant.

The MIS/DP department's responsibility at PolyBak is similar to that of MIS/DP in any other large corporation, except that it also handles in-house imaging. The paper flow inside the company has been reduced to nearly nil by imaging (scanning) documents as they enter the company and handling them only in their electronic form until they leave the company.

PolyBak also houses an aggressive Treasury department that generates substantial revenues for the company via astutely timed currency conversions, expertly managed cash, and prudent investing.

Project Background

The company's vice president for manufacturing, the sponsor of our work, contacted us several weeks ago to ask about expert systems. He requested information on how to discover areas in which expert systems might be applied to increase productivity, distribute knowledge more widely, and improve quality. We explained the Users' Dissatisfaction List and the Managers' Wish List (see Chapter 3 "Prospecting") and sent him brief synopses of projects we had done in several related domains (in several paradigms and with several purposes). We hoped that these criteria and examples would help him focus his search for applications inside the company before we arrived to discuss his situation.

Last week, the Manufacturing VP met with his CEO, the other VPs, and the managers of the groups under his direction (in separate meetings) to determine where expert systems might be introduced. We will be speaking with people from the departments identified in those meetings as possible sites for expert systems.

We began today's series of meetings with the Manufacturing VP and people from all the departments we will be prospecting in. The Manufacturing VP called the meeting to publicly assure us of his support for our projects and to instruct the groups in his charge to suspend their ordinary daily routine in order to cooperate with us in our task of prospecting for appropriate applications. He has informed us and his staff that "all doors are open" to us.

We had asked to meet separately with representatives from all groups that may have a use for expert systems, in order to discover areas of application suitable for development. So a full slate of meetings has been arranged for us. We will not be meeting with the groups in any particular order; meetings were set up according to the schedules of the participants. We hope to finish this preliminary prospecting in one day.

Our first substantive meeting is with Cydney, Duncan, and Marlin of the Treasury department. The woman and the two men, all in their thirties, are formally attired, but casual and comfortable in their mannerisms. They each take a seat and produce notebooks and pens. After introductions, we offer a brief synopsis of what expert systems are and what they do, indicating possible uses in a Treasury department. We do this in case the participants have only been told to appear at the meeting ready to discuss expert systems in general.

But we are encouraged when Cydney begins a technical discussion of the Treasury department's expert system needs right away.

Cydney:

"What we're interested in, first, is a system to provide us with investment advice. And we need it to operate when the investor's back is turned.

"The investor is very busy. All our people are very busy. And sometimes that ends up in mistakes. A few days ago, we meant to write a contract for—what was it?—150 million lire? And it was written for 150 contracts in lire instead. Before we noticed it, we'd lost more than everybody in this room makes in a year—in one day. So we'd eventually like to make a system that could catch obvious mistakes and transcription errors like that. But first we're looking at investment advice as a higher payoff."

Two separate systems were just mentioned: one to attend to lapses of attention, the other to offer investment recommendations.

"We want to take advantage of opportunities that may be escaping the notice of the investor because he's preoccupied or she's preoccupied.

"What we want to do—what we were hoping a knowledge-based system could do...."

Interesting. At no time have we used the term "knowledge-based system" in our discussions with anyone in this company. We've referred only to "expert systems." So this group has been reading about the field on their own—a good sign.

"What we want is an expert system that can [reading off of a sheet of paper]:

"One. Analyze and portray trends in pricing based on rate feed data to the investor early in the morning, to serve as the basis for a day's investment decisions."

"Rate feed data" have to come from somewhere. This will probably be an integration link that will be required before the expert system can be useful.

"Two. Make recommendations on which investment to make at a particular time, an explanation of why the recommendation is being given, what the term of the investment should be, and some kind of warning of potential problems if the investor decides not to take the system's recommendations.

"For the moment, we thought we'd concentrate on U.S. investments before foreign."

We are taking these requests down in a notebook, but will ask for a copy of Cydney's sheet after the meeting as well.

What has been stated is that the expert system should make investment recommendations, but no indication of what information the investors use to make their recommendations has surfaced yet. So, an unbounded domain is a possibility if the investors use not only models, charts, and technical experience, but also such difficult-to-analyze data as news reports. We'll have to investigate the data that the investors use to make their decisions.

Also, we'll need to discover what types of models and spreadsheets they have at present. We will probably have to tie into them eventually. That may present some integration challenges.

"Three. We want to flag hot prospects and warn the investor about dangerous circumstances that arise during the day as the investor is working, based on the expert system's knowledge of the portfolio and the market. These would be recommendations made without input from the investor. They'd be volunteered spontaneously by the system whenever it had something to report on.

"And four. Make a recommendation any time the investor asks for it."

KE:

"You mentioned a feed. Where does the data that the investors analyze come from?"

Marlin:

"Most of it comes over Telexate. But some of it comes from London Winterbank, the bid and asked. And we have a homemade spreadsheet application called Treasury Invest that we use for portfolio maintenance."

KE:

"For the system to be useful, you'd need all three of those links made. You'd need the expert system to take or return data from those three sources."

Marlin:

"Yes. Take data from Telexate and London. Take and return data to the spreadsheet. It would also have to take into account international tax situations and things like time deposits not being acceptable beyond six months, legal limits, investment guidelines for each bank, portfolio requirements, company policy, yields, what's in the portfolios at the time of investment, bank acceptability and availability, things like that."

Writing these down quickly. They may serve as a basis for later knowledge acquisition. This also does seem to hint that investment decisions are made chiefly on the basis of technical factors, so unbounded domain may be less of a problem than anticipated.

Duncan:

"And if you get all that done by next week," he says smiling, "we have another project we've been hatching lately. We're not sure it can be done. But let me explain what it is, and you say if it's feasible.

"What we want to create is a wholesale pricing competitive analysis system. Every week we establish wholesale prices for our various products. We have about 30 products now, different kinds of packaging that we sell. Our customers have plenty of companies to choose from, as you know. So, we readjust our wholesale prices every week to keep them competitive without cutting into margins. We never low-ball. We never put the price so low that we're losing money just to gain market share.

"The prices are set weekly at all of our wholesale locations around the world, based on an analysis of market forces, our company objectives, past and anticipated pricing actions of competitors, and—obviously—profit margin considerations.

"We've been collecting historical pricing data on our competitors for years, but we never really consult the data because the quantity is just overwhelming. But this year we would like to incorporate the analysis of historical competitors' price data into our weekly analysis task.

"We were kind of hoping an expert system could help us with this. We'd want it, eventually, to be able to offer price-setting recommendations based on its understanding of the price-setting patterns of our competitors. See, we're trying to figure out how they'll set their prices so we can set ours just a hair lower every time."

KE:

Repeating what we think we've just understood.

"So, you want to try to produce an expert system that, to some degree, will induce or predict the behavior of your competitors in a particular market circumstance for a particular product in a given week and make a suggestion as to what you should do in that circumstance—for example, recommend that you lower your price—based on its understanding of the other competitors.

"And the way you want to figure out what your competitors are doing is by studying all the historical pricing data and seeing if there are any patterns in there that you can use to understand how the competitors are setting their prices. At the moment, there are no experts in this field in your company, so you essentially want to create an expert by analyzing the data. Is that it?"

Marlin:

"That's it."

This is an inductive system. Not a good candidate for a first expert system. Better to begin with a deductive one, then move on to induction when they are comfortable with how expert systems work. But a fascinating project.

The inductive system's return on investment would accrue over the course of many weeks. Small savings or increases in profit would add up over many separate decisions by the expert system. The investment advisor's return on investment might also accrue over many weeks, or it might point out a single investment opportunity missed by the investors and earn its keep in a single transaction. The third system suggested, the anomaly detection system to catch currency order mistakes before they are committed, would pay for itself by catching a few large transaction errors.

The first system for this particular group should be the investment advisor (because it is deductive and has a high rate of return), but because of all of its integration requirements, that system may not be at the top of the whole company's list of expert systems to develop. A better first system would require fewer integration links while still offering a high return on investment.

We'll continue looking for a good first project.

Our next meeting is with Willaby, manager of the MIS group, the group that will be responsible for maintaining and supporting the finished expert systems that we develop.

It is unusual to have only a single person from a group attend this kind of meeting. Other people in a group often ask to attend, out of curiosity or to protect themselves if they believe any work will be assigned during the meeting. Or several experts who work together may all attend together. When one person attends alone, usually it signals one of four situations:

- *He or she has just recently been contacted about participating and is showing up for what is believed to be an ad hoc meeting.*

- *The group is very small and one person can adequately represent the group.*

- *The other people in the group are too valuable to spare for this kind of meeting.*

- *The person would like to discuss projects out of earshot of the other members of the group.*

  We suspect the last case.

Willaby:

"Let's get right to the heart of the problem, okay? I have too many business analysts in my organization. Anything you can do to help me reduce their number would be great. I'd like to automate their jobs.

"The business analysts translate what the users say they want into program specs. They look at three things: how big the project's going to be, how many people will have to work on the thing, and what has to be done in the code. They use five regular metrics for speccing out the problem: size, scale, schedule, personnel, and risks/benefits."

Size apparently means code volume, the number of lines of code needed to automate each task requested by the system users.

Scale must be a description or definition of each of the functions to be encoded into the system and an idea of how big the finished system has to be.

Schedule would be the length of time necessary to encode each portion of the system.

Personnel probably means deciding how many programmers will be assigned to each program module.

And risk/benefit analysis must be determining whether the cost of building the system will be less than the cost of user inefficiency and lost productivity that would result from not building the system.

"I want you to build an expert system for me that does the analysts' job. Then I'll give it to the programmers and they can do their own jobs and the analysts' jobs at the same time."

KE:

"But will the analysts cooperate when they discover that they're helping to create a system that replaces them?"

Willaby:

"They're free to leave anytime."

That's all we need to hear. There is no system here. A deductive system for this task would require cooperative experts. And an inductive system is not appropriate since experts and domain knowledge exist. In all other ways, this would be an ideal project: experts exist, their skill is rare and costly, their expertise is based on experience, and they represent a bottleneck or chokepoint for the organization. But we can't build a system to replace people behind their backs or against their wills. Even attempting to build such a system would poison the entire organization with fear and anger. Until some appropriate incentive is found to motivate the analysts, we'll pass this system by.

The meeting with Willaby continues long enough to discover if any other possiblities exist in the MIS group. (There are none.) We explain that trying to clone the analysts without their knowledge or agreement is courting expensive disaster.

Our next meeting is with Desdemona and Cyril, managers of the Shipping/Distribution group. Desdemona has been with the company for 18 years, Cyril for 9. Both have been informed about the kinds of projects we're looking for.

We've been told unofficially that Desdemona knows and is liked by everyone in the company, has done every job there is, is highly respected for her candor, honesty, and intelligence, is turned to by the VPs in every emergency, is someone we will enjoy talking with, and is likely to be the next vice president, possibly the next CEO. A glowing recommendation. So we're looking forward to reviewing the company's political structure with a respected veteran employee as we prospect for possible expert systems.

Desdemona:

"You're working with Rory? The Manufacturing VP? He's good. He just got that job, you know. He was way over in Corporate before. He got dragged into the Manufacturing job because he has a good reputation, and the Manufacturing group has been having some difficulties lately. So now Rory has to try to fix them. That'll teach him to do good work." She laughs.

"Have you met with everyone else yet? No? Oh, Treasury and MIS? How did you like Willaby?" She laughs again. "He was probably glad to see you folks, because no one else will talk to him. He's actually a nice guy and a first-rate manager. But he seems to be alienating his people by moving so fast. At the request of his boss—we have kind of an informal management system here—I'm scheduled to meet with him this afternoon to discuss morale.

"Maybe we should tell you a little about what else you're going to find in the different groups. Just so you know what's going on. This is a great company to work for, but I've been here 18 years, and nobody knows the troubles I've seen." She laughs.

"We've got all kinds of interesting problems, if that's what you're looking for. But most of them don't have anything to do with technology. And some of them you're going to run right smack into. So you're going to have to be careful in a few departments because you'll be walking into quicksand.

"The Systems Implementation group is in the middle of a reorganization, so you probably won't get to talk with them today. But in six months or so, you should arrange some interviews with them—after they find their feet.

"And just so you know, you should steer away from Winslow in Paper Product Manufacturing for an expert because he and Rory don't get along—even though you're going to want to work with him when you meet him. He's been with the company since Methuselah was a baby. But he and Rory've been at odds for years, and right now Rory's got the upper hand, so stay away from Winslow—even though he's a great person and the one who knows the most of anyone in that group.

"Jacques in Resin Manufacture is perfect, though. You should definitely talk with him. But don't approach Sybil in Resin Package Production if you also want to work with Spider in Paper Packaging,

---

because those groups are in the middle of a big power struggle. And believe me, you don't want to get caught in the middle of all that by appearing to favor one expert over another.

"Otherwise, all doors are open!" she exclaims laughing.

Hmmm. Well. Here we have just discovered the difference between building an academic expert system and building a commercial expert system. The commercial world is more politically complex. And politics can aid or hinder the development of an expert system (something a KE has to keep in mind).

Cyril:

"Anything else you want to know?"

KE:

"Well. I see you have some of the explanatory information we handed out about what expert systems are and how they work. Do you have any ideas for projects we might pursue in your group?"

Cyril:

"We've been thinking about it. But I think the problems we have here are small potatoes compared to the ones in the other groups, because we're so exceptionally talented and capable here." He laughs. "If you don't strike any pay dirt in the other groups, come back to us. Maybe we'll have something by then."

No expert systems here yet. But the political information is invaluable and has been scribbled into the prospecting notebook.

The next meeting is with Tobias, Kazuto, Glee, and Jacques from the Resin Film Manufacture group. They have responsibility for the manufacture of the uncut resin film.

Jacques was spoken of favorably by Desdemona.

Tobias:

"Hi. How are you? In your handout here, it says we should ask ourselves 'Where does it hurt the most?' Well, we have a big pain in Scheduling and it's getting worse." Jacques starts laughing. The others smile. "So, that's one place we'd like to try to get some help in. Think you could do anything about that?

"Okay, well, Jacques's the problem."

Tobias and Jacques are smiling. Jacques is in his early sixties, Tobias his early fifties. They are evidently friends.

"Or maybe I'm the problem because I can't figure out what he does. When he retires next year, all our scheduling will go out the window. It took 14 years in the paper plant to master the job, and then three years in Resin to perfect all his secret techniques. And we've got no one to put in his place. We've trained three, that's three, people to take over. One of them moved. One of them got promoted out of the plant. And the third one is leaving next month and isn't coming back. And the number of products we make—products that'll have to be scheduled— will increase 50% this year. And we have a new plant opening in eight months with no scheduler in it. So we're up the creek when Jacques leaves. If we want to solve this problem, we have to get moving soon."

KE:

"What you need is another Jacques? Or at least Jacques's knowledge in the computer?"

Kazuto:

"Yes. And we would like to call it "Jacques in the Box." Everyone laughs.

Sounds fruitful so far. A proxy system would be the goal—to replace the retiring expert—but an advisory system to help a novice scheduler might be a usable first step. The expert is evidently willing. They have tried other methods of solving the problem but without success. Time to investigate some parameters of the problem to flush out any obvious technical snags.

KE:

"What exactly is involved in 'scheduling'? You're scheduling the production of resin film according to what the customers have ordered?"

Jacques:

"Yes, that's right. The film machines produce the film we sell for packaging. The machines produce a lot of different products. And sometimes the film is dyed black or red or green or white, or it's just left opaque. There are different thicknesses of film and different due dates for every lot. Some machines do only certain thicknesses of film. And we can't make white film after black film because the black dye taints the white, so we end up with grey for the first hundred feet, and we have to throw it out. There's no solid waste problem because we can just use it for mulch—sometimes we take it home for the garden— but I've lost the time I could have used making the right color film if it comes out grey. And the customer won't take grey if he ordered white."

Scribbling furiously. We usually don't bring tape recorders until after prospecting has finished and acquisition has begun. But occasionally during prospecting, a lot of useful domain knowledge spills out in a disorganized gush. So we write quickly to try to capture it while it's fresh. This allows us to begin thinking about what knowledge we'll need to collect during acquisition sessions later on. Scribbled notes now include: "Film. Constraints: Colors: black, white, red, green, etc. Thicknesses: vary. Machines: only certain thicknesses, colors in sequence." This arcane scrawl may or may not make sense when viewed several days from now. But it's a start and will allow us to at least prompt the expert during acquisition.

This appears to be the best of the five possible expert systems considered so far. Return on investment is high. The organization and the expert are well motivated. The knowledge about scheduling the production of different resins seems to depend on factors that could be encoded into an expert system. This should be the first system to recommend.

Knowledge Acquisition

We have presented our findings in a written report to the Manufacturing VP and have waited for funding. When given the go ahead, we set up another meeting with Jacques, the domain expert, to begin knowledge acquisition for the resin film scheduling system, the system we've chosen to tackle first.

The first knowledge acquisition meeting is held in a room next to Jacques's office. We want him to feel comfortable with the surroundings, so the meeting is held on his home ground. But we also want to remove him from any cues or props (such as calendars, calculators, or scribbled mnemonics) he may unconsciously use in his own office when making scheduling decisions. And we want to remove him from the ringing telephone in his office.

We have agreed to meet in this room for an hour each week on this day. A terminal will be brought in for prototype demonstrations, which should begin in three weeks.

KE:

"Can you briefly describe your job, so we can get an understanding of what kinds of abilities the expert system should have?"

Jacques:

"Every day a new batch of orders for certain kinds of films comes in. Some of them are rush jobs, so we do those emergency orders first. That sets back the other orders, and I have to reshuffle the schedule to make sure no one's order gets pushed back beyond its due date."

Emergency orders are, evidently, exceptions in the ordinary scheme of scheduling.

"Only certain machines can run certain kinds of orders—they can make only certain kinds of film. We have 62 machines on the floor. But some of them can only handle resin that's 1 millimeter to 3 millimeters thick. So, they can't handle all the orders we get. Some machines can only handle .4 to .7 millimeter resin. So we have to put the orders on the machines that can handle them."

As soon as we hear "can only" and "have to," we think of constraints. The orders are constrained to be finished by a certain due date. And the machines are constrained to process only certain types of orders.

"Some orders are for white film. We try to do all those together, so we don't have to clean out the machine between orders. We can run a black or red order after white because the colored dye just overwhelms the white dye. But we can't run white after black or a color without cleaning out the machine. That takes time, so we'd like to avoid that if possible.

"My job is to arrange the orders so that: they all get done before they are due, and we switch colors as few times as possible, and we do the regular scheduled maintenance, and we do the emergency orders as they come in, and all 62 machines are producing, and no people or hardware are lying idle. It's juggling."

After orders have been constrained to certain machines, they must then be arranged into some sequence, for example, all red orders together. So there are two pieces to this system: constraints to tell us

---

*which films can be made on which machines, and rules to tell us
how to group constrained orders together (for example, all red-dye
film orders in a row).*

KE:

"Can you show me what a typical schedule looks like and how you
arrive at it?"

Jacques:

[Holding out a sheet of graph paper blocked off according to orders
and machines] "Here's today's schedule. Mondays are usually the
slowest day, so this is a good day for us to meet. But next time I'll bring
some more difficult end-of-the-week schedules to show you.

"Each of these long rows is one machine's schedule. The filled-in
boxes are the orders scheduled on that machine. The numbers in the
boxes tell you what order is scheduled there.

"If you look up on this order list over here, you see that order number
766 is for 2-millimeter-thick red resin. It has a granularity of .06. It's
not coated. It's made with resin type 3. It will be used for food
packaging. It is due on this date. We have to make 1000 linear feet of
it. And here's the customer's name.

"Now I put that order on machine 32, because 32 handles any
thickness between 1 and 7 millimeters, and it ran three red orders just
before this, so we wouldn't have to clean out the machine to run it. I
couldn't put this order on something like machine 54 here, even though
it has almost all red resin on it, because 54 can't make film for food
packaging. And this order is for food film. And I put this guy after the
other red orders on this machine, not before them, because it has a later
due date than they do. But I put it before this other red order here
because 1000-linear-feet orders always go before smaller orders. Got
all that?"

KE:

"So, let's see." *Time to map out the variables.* "A machine can handle
film of a certain thickness, color, granularity, coating, resin type, use,
length, and customer. Is that right?"

Jacques:

"Well. Any machine can handle any length and any customer. But the rest of those things depend on what the machine can handle. Right."

So, "length" and "customer" are attributes of an order. But they are not constraints to be used in scheduling the order.

KE:

"And an order can have a certain thickness, color, due date, all of those things. And you match the orders with particular characteristics to the machines that can handle them."

Jacques:

"Right. But it's not just machines and orders. Some things can't be done on certain days. Like we can't do regularly scheduled maintenance on Saturdays or Sundays because the union doesn't allow it. And if it's a holiday, we want to run no jobs at all if possible, or just the top priority jobs, so we can get in here and out fast, or not come in at all."

KE:

"Can you give me a list of all 62 machines, describing what kinds of orders they can handle? And a bunch of old orders? That would get me started."

Jacques:

"No problem."

Knowledge Representation

Using the list of machine characteristics and three sample orders as references, we begin thinking about knowledge representation. And we start with what we know about scheduling applications in general.

Most scheduling/planning systems are composed of two components:

- a set of constraints and heuristics that dictate how new information is handled

- new information (orders or things to be scheduled) mapped against those constraints and sequencing rules

---

A constraint, for example, may be "Green film cannot be made on machine #47." A heuristic used to arrange orders may be "A red film order should be made immediately after another red film order whenever possible."

A piece of new information (an order to be scheduled) might be

"Make

100,000 linear feet

of white film

of thickness 0.7 mm

by next Friday."

The scheduling expert system applies the new order information against all the constraints and heuristics and all the other information the system has (other orders and other constraints, for example, no orders started during lunch hour) to decide when to perform the new request. This can be done in two steps.

In step 1, the orders are measured against the constraints, and lists are created of all the orders that could possibly be handled by each machine (many orders could probably be handled by more than one machine). This, in a sense, is a first cut at scheduling the orders, because it eliminates all combinations of order and machine except the ones allowed by the constraints. It shows all the ways in which the order could be fulfilled. For example, an order for blue 0.7 mm film could be made on machine #3 or machine #44 (because those machines allow the manufacture of blue 0.7 mm film).

Step 2 involves comparing the possible orders for one machine against the possible orders for other machines. For example, if machine #3 must be used to process other orders of higher priority, only machine #44 can be used for this order of blue 0.7 mm film. Then this blue 0.7 mm film order is compared to the other orders that could be done on machine #44.

The second step often requires the assignment of sequencing priorities. If film type 83 can be made only on machine #44 then an order to make film type 83 has higher priority on machine #44 than an order for a film type that can be made on machine #1, #2, #3, or #44. And if there are two orders for film type 83, then the order with the soonest due date has the highest priority on machine #83. The orders with the lowest priority on each machine are changed first when two orders conflict. In the end, a final schedule appears.

Coding

When beginning to build a scheduling expert system, a KE looks at the same three components all programmers study: input, output, and processing.

Output is the finished schedule. It may take the form of a schematic of a telecomm network with loads represented as lines of various thicknesses between nodes (exchanges). Or the output may be a map of a natural gas pipeline with colors designating flow rates or products. But usually the output is a horizontal bar graph. In this case, each bar represents the orders on a single machine. For example:

DAY

MACHINE	1	2	3	4	5	6	7	8	9	10	11	12	13
1	[order 2] [order 7] [order 99]
2	[order 64] [order 22] [order 117]
3	[order 1198] [order 1] [order 9879]
4	[order 9827] [order 90] [order 234]

Processing is the way in which scheduling decisions are made, usually by applying constraints to new orders and then sequencing the constrained orders.

In this case, processing will involve at least three, perhaps four, components:

- orders (things to be scheduled)

- machine constraints (limitations on scheduling certain orders)

- sequencing instructions (detailing the priority of orders on machines)

- cost considerations (optional)

These three (or four) parts together are used to determine when and where orders will be scheduled.

Input to the finished system will be only new orders.

Constraints, orders, and priorities can be viewed as either objects or rules.

An object constraint can describe, for example, a machine's limitations:

Class: machines

Object: machine #7

Attribute: resin-types-allowed

Value: type-x, type-y, type-z

Attribute: film-widths-allowed-in-mms

Value: 0.2 - 0.9

Attribute: how-often-maintenance-is-required-in-days

Value: 10

Attribute: colors-allowed

Value: white, grey, green

Attribute: time-since-last-maintenance-in-days

Value: 2

Orders also can be input as objects:

Class: film-orders

Object: order #1

Attribute: priority

Value: emergency

Attribute: color

Value: white

Attribute: type

Value: type-x

Attribute: due-date

Value: August-1

Attribute: width-in-mms

Value: 0.24

Attribute: days-to-process

Value: 3

The system, via rules, is then shown which machine constraint attributes and order attributes map together, for example:

Machine: *film-types-allowed*—Order: *type*

Machine: *film-widths-allowed-in-mms*—Order: *width-in-mms*

Machine: *colors-allowed*—Order: *color*

This means we create a rule that compares orders and constraints:

```
If
order-name = [order-name]
     type = [type]
     width-in-mms = [width-in-mms]
     color = [color]
and
machine-name = [machine-name]
     film-types-allowed = [type]
     film-widths-allowed-in-mms = [width-in-mms]
     colors-allowed = [color]
then
order-name = [order-name] can be placed on
machine-name = [machine-name]
```

When the program is run, the order and machine objects that are passed through this rule result in a long list of orders that could be fulfilled on particular machines, for example,

possible match: machine #7, order #15

possible match: machine #7, order #17

possible match: machine #7, order #1

possible match: machine #3, order #15

possible match: machine #3, order #26

possible match: machine #3, order #9

Sequencing priorities (heuristics) then are used to filter (to schedule, to arrange) the possible matches. Earliest due dates, for example, may cause an order to become highest priority among a group of possible orders for one machine. A particular order may also be designated a "rush" or "emergency" order and thus scheduled first.

Priorities are set by the programmer in rules that establish which order, machine, or other characteristic is most important in deciding the sequence in which orders will be handled on a machine. Or an object containing a list of priorities for all machines may be read by the rules to sequence orders. Such an object might list priorities in order of importance or assign numerical figures to each to signify their importance in sequencing orders. For example,

Priority: Emergency

Colors-allowed: Green

Colors-allowed: Grey

Colors-allowed: Black

Film-widths-allowed-in-mms: 0.1 - 0.7

Time-since-last-maintenance:

(Time-since-last-maintenance + days-to-process)

=10

What this list would mean is that Priority:Emergency orders would be scheduled first when there were several possible orders that could be put on a machine. Then all Color:Green orders would be scheduled, then all Color:Grey orders, and so on. Eventually this kind of sequencing list could be created not only for all machines as a group in the shop but for *each separate machine* as well.

Prototyping and Delivery

Our first prototype, delivered after three weeks, does nothing more than map order characteristics to machine constraints. It produces a list that shows which current orders could possibly be handled on which machines, for example:

Machine 1: Order 27, Order 889, Order 451, Order 321, Order 334

Machine 2: Order 889, Order 68, Order 27, Order 990, Order 7

Though it is small, the system is already of some use to the expert, who asks to have it installed on his own workstation. It will at least save him the time spent matching machines to orders and thereby reduce his workload. This tiny prototype (62 objects—one for each machine on the shop floor—and 11 rules) becomes the first frozen version of the system.

The next prototypes progressively refine the task of sequencing the orders: deciding which orders have higher priority on each machine. The output for the next frozen prototype (62 objects, 71 rules—most rules having to do with sequencing orders on machines) shows the same list of orders, but arranged according to priority on each machine, for example:

Machine 1: Order 451, Order 334, Order 321, Order 27, Order 889

Machine 2: Order 889, Order 990, Order 7, Order 27, Order 68

In all prototypes thus far, no dates have been taken into consideration. The orders have been placed on machines and arranged regardless of their due dates. So, the next versions of the expert system address this problem:

Machine 1: Order 451, Order 334, Order 321 (total: 8 days)

Machine 2: Order 889, Order 990, Order 7, Order 27
(total: 8 days)

What we find during this long prototyping process is that prototyping an expert system is not like building a house. It is like painting a portrait. A house builder must adhere strictly to the blueprints. Architectural drawings are not merely guidelines; they are denotations of the way in which the house must be built. Any substitution of materials, approximation of measurements, or deviation from the plans jeopardizes the eventual stability and functionality of the house. And the plans must be followed in strict sequence (walls cannot be ripped out to put in electrical wiring or plumbing).

But for the painter, a rough sketch—a prototype—becomes a clean drawing—another prototype—that then acts only as a guide for the addition of color to the canvas. An ear can be removed with turpentine and repainted after the face is in. And the act of rendering an accurate but flattering portrayal of the subject is one of successive approximation toward a final goal, not scrupulous planning followed by unswerving implementation.

The consequences of not adhering to the plan are also different in each case. If the finished house deviates significantly from the intended plan, the builder's implementation of the plan is judged to be faulty and inadequate; the edifice may keel over as a result. But if the finished portrait deviates from the sketch, it is the sketch that is recognized as inadequate. And the painting is better, not worse, for having deviated from the plan. So it is with expert systems, which evolve

---

The final major changes to the knowledgebase (after four months of
prototyping) include the addition of rules that group separate orders
into lots according to similar color or type. After this modification (total
now: 68 objects, 170 rules), the graphical backend is tackled.

The graphical backend allows the scheduler to see the schedules for
all machines and all orders. It is almost identical in appearance to the
sheet of graph paper the scheduler has used for so many years, except
that the edges of the graph are almost infinitely extensible by length
and width to incorporate all orders for each machine for three months,
with up to 200 machines being scheduled. The graphical backend is
linked to the expert system via a conventional language interface
program that takes data from the expert system and deposits them in
the graphical backend's buffers.

At last, six months after the first knowledge acquisition interviews,
the final version of the expert system is delivered whole to the expert.
It is used in parallel with the expert for several months and is then
declared "safe" for use.

*We are lucky in this case that we're working in the scheduling
paradigm, because the cycle of testing and acceptance for scheduling
systems is relatively straightforward. After prototyping (once we
believe we have encoded all necessary constraints and sequencing
rules), we give the system historical orders to chew on. The schedule
created by the system is then matched against the schedule that was
created by hand for those same orders.*

*When the schedule the system creates fails to match the expert's
schedule, the difference is often glaring (a dozen orders put on the
wrong machine). But generally we find that the orders were placed
on wrong machines for one of two reasons:*

- *all orders were misdirected because of one cause (for example,
  we did not know that 0.3-0.7mm machines could also handle
  0.9mm film: a constraint the expert had forgotten to mention)*

- *one order was misdirected to the wrong machine (for example,
  because it had a granularity type we had never seen before: a new
  attribute-value pair previously unknown to us) and all other
  orders just rearranged themselves around this errant order*

In time, the system-created schedules directly match the human-made schedules (or they differ slightly in ways that the expert does not object to), and we begin live parallel testing of the system (with both expert and expert system creating daily schedules).

Other paradigms have different testing and acceptance cycles, however—the longest and most difficult being that of the Monitoring/Anomaly Detection system (the type of system used to catch the attention lapses of foreign currency traders, for example). Such systems often are tested extensively and then fielded in parallel with the experts they are meant to mimic or second-guess. But when first introduced to a group that has never had to look at an expert system's results before— a group that need not look at the system to continue its operations—the system is frequently ignored.

After several weeks of apparent abandonment, someone from the backroom is assigned to actually sit in front of the terminal to watch the expert system's recommendations appear on the screen. This person initially announces the system's recommendations to the group aloud as they happen, but demurs after noticing that the experts have already acted in accordance with the recommendations before they have been announced.

This painful situation continues until the day when the system announces a recommendation that none of the experts appears to be implementing. The person watching the screen meekly suggests, in a whisper, that the experts please look at the effect of factor X on factor Y, noting that the expert system suggests this is an opportunity worth acting on immediately. This request is shrugged off by all but one expert who glances at a screen, realizes the opportunity does exist, and capitalizes on it quickly, thereby making or saving the organization enough money in a single transaction to pay for all expert system development in the group in perpetuity.

The next morning at 8 a.m., all the experts are huddled around the screen, muttering, "Well, what does it say now?" And that situation continues until the expert system (whose knowledgebase is not yet perfected) makes a mistake. The cycle of abandonment and enthrallment then begins anew.

Epilog

After the scheduling system is up and running on a daily basis, discussion begins on how to extend or modify the program to incorporate machines in other plants, especially the newly built plant that has no official scheduler assigned to it yet.

After Jacques in the Box has been declared fully and independently operational and successful, meetings are held to discuss the investor advisor system for the PolyBak Treasury department.

Tool Selection   *B*

The Knowledge Engineer as Arbiter

A KE should consider the following factors when choosing an expert system development tool or language:

- Availability and cost of the tool.

- Execution performance (the runtime speed of the tool), especially for realtime applications.

- User interface friendliness, especially for high-volume applications with naive users.

- Hardware/software requisites (the hardware or software required for the tool's use).

- Problem paradigm needs. For example, diagnostic, anomaly detective, and analytic systems often require a tool to backward chain (find a solution quickly with a minimum of data). Configuration and scheduling systems often require forward chaining (the collection of copious data before making a decision). Anomaly detection and pattern recognition systems often require realtime speed.

- Dimensions of the knowledgebase, including constraints on the number or size of objects/frames/rules or on general code volume.

- Complexity of knowledge representation and modeling requirements

- flexibility of the tool's inference and inheritance methods (for example, backward and forward chaining in same application)
- knowledge representation and user interface restrictions (for example, O-V pairs only or lack of rule-based iconic manipulation)

- Development/knowledge engineering interface, including

  - functionality of the knowledgebase editor
  - ease of debugging
  - openness of the tool's architecture
  - its development interface (separate from its user interface)
  - ease of viewing/manipulating the knowledgebase

- Support, that is, the degree of training and the experience level of KEs necessary before the tool can be put to best use.

- Integration abilities, that is, the requirements for linkage and the ease with which that linkage to other hardwares, databases, conventional systems, languages, or expert systems can be made.

Knowledge Engineer Selection

C

The Knowledge Engineer as Team Builder

KEs who are building a team of KEs for expert system development projects often interview applicants with an eye toward finding the most technically qualified people who will also be able to work well with domain experts, funders, managers, and users. The following questions frequently are asked when a KE is interviewing other prospective KEs.

Experience

Has this person actually built an expert system? Or have they only done prospecting, tool selection, user interfaces, project management (unless a manager is what is being sought), or some other ancillary task?

How much of the expert system listed on the resume did this person actually code?

Has this person worked in most levels of expert system development? Or only at the design level, leaving the rest of the system for other people to finish? (The answer might indicate lack of knowledge or concern about production level work.)

Has this person's expert systems solved real-world problems, or were they only toys?

Technical Abilities

Can this person code (in AI languages/tools)?
Is this person acquainted with expert systems in general, such as:

- knowledge representation schemes (for example, rules, frames/objects, semantic nets, logic, cases)

- knowledge engineering tasks (for example, prospecting, acquisition/elicitation, design, prototyping, coding, expectations management, teaching)

- methods of inference (for example, forward and backward deduction, induction)

- expert system application paradigms (for example, diagnosis, interpretation, anomaly detection, scheduling/planning, prediction)

- areas of interest bordering expert systems (for example, ICAI, CIM, CAD, hybrid systems, machine learning)

- knowledge of particular domains (for example, financial services, manufacturing, telecommunications)

Fit

Is this person a chemist, a civil engineer, or a CPA who is dabbling in AI? Or a KE who happens to have experience in a particular domain?
Would they rather be a researcher? Or a tool builder? Or in natural language? Or not building commercial applications?

Personality

Could this person be put in front of a customer? Could we work with this person?

Attitude/Motivation

Does this person seem enthusiatic about (or at least interested in) AI, knowledge engineering, and doing the kind of work we do?

Travel

Could this person travel to other sites at the rate we travel?

General

Is this person intelligent, articulate, a self-starter?
Does this person seem willing to learn, grow, expand?
Why is this person leaving his/her last job?
Are there any particular areas in AI of special interest to this person (possible contributions to the group)?
Does this person have some special domain knowledge that we could use?
Does this person have any questions about what we do?
Is this a junior-level or senior-level person?

Three Broad Questions to Ponder

Can this person do the kind of work we require? (Ability)
Have they done the kind of work we require? (Experience)
Do they want to do the kind of work we require? (Fit)

Some Possible Leading Questions

"Which parts of this expert system did you work on?" or "What was your role in this project?"

"How did you find working with Prolog (or Nexpert, OPS5, LISP or whatever tools/languages you've worked with)?"

"If you consider the whole spectrum of tasks in knowledge engineering, from prospecting, design, and the initiation of expert systems to actual knowledge representation, coding, and implementation to project management, where do you see yourself?"

Bibliography

Introductory Texts

Addis, T. R. *Designing Knowledge-Based Systems.* Englewood Cliffs, NJ: Prentice Hall, Inc., 1985.

Bahrami, A. *Designing Artificial Intelligence Based Software.* New York: Halsted Press, 1988.

Bartee, Thomas C., ed. *Expert Systems and Artificial Intelligence.* Indianapolis, IN: Howard W. Sams & Company, 1988.

Buchanan, Bruce G., and Shortliffe, Edward. *Rule-Based Expert Systems.* Reading, MA: Addison-Wesley Publishing Co., Inc., 1984.

Charniak, Eugene. *Artificial Intelligence Programming.* Hillsdale, NJ: Lawrence Erlbaum Associates, 1987.

Charniak, Eugene, and McDermott, Drew. *Introduction to Artificial Intelligence.* Reading, MA: Addison-Wesley Publishing Co., Inc., 1985.

Frost, Richard. *Introduction to Knowledge Based Systems.* Riverside, NJ: Macmillan, Inc., 1986.

Goodall, Alex. *The Guide to Expert Systems.* Medford, NJ: Learned Information Ltd., 1985.

Gupta, Amar, and Presad, Bandreddi E., eds. *Principles of Expert Systems.* New York: IEEE Press, 1988.

Harmon, Paul, and King, David. *Expert Systems: Artificial Intelligence in Business.* New York: John Wiley and Sons, Inc., 1985.

Jackson, Peter. *Introduction to Expert Systems.* Reading, MA: Addison-Wesley Publishing Co., Inc., 1986.

Keller, Robert. *Expert System Technology: Development and Application.* Englewood Cliffs, NJ: Prentice Hall, Inc., 1987.

Lenat, Douglas, and Davis, Randall. *Knowledge-Based Systems in Artificial Intelligence.* New York: McGraw-Hill, Inc. 1982.

Luger, George F. *Artificial Intelligence and the Design of Expert Systems.* Menlo Park, CA: Benjamin Cummings, 1989.

Nilsson, Nils J. *Principles of Artificial Intelligence.* Palo Alto, CA: Tioga Press, 1980.

Parsaye, Kamran, and Chignell, Mark. *Expert Systems for Experts.* New York: John Wiley and Sons, 1988.

Rich, Elaine. *Artificial Intelligence.* New York: McGraw-Hill, Inc., 1983.

Rolston, David W. *Principles of Artificial Intelligence and Expert Systems Development.* New York: McGraw-Hill, Inc., 1988.

Savory, Stuart E., ed. *Expert Systems in the Organization: An Introduction for Decision-Makers.* Chichester, UK: Ellis Horwood, 1988.

Schank, Roger. *The Cognitive Computer.* Reading, MA: Addison-Wesley Publishing Co., Inc., 1984.

Sharples, Mike, et al. *Computers and Thought: A Practical Introduction to Artificial Intelligence.* Cambridge, MA: MIT Press, 1989.

Shiria, Yoshiaki, and Tsujii, Jun-ichi. *Artificial Intelligence: Concepts, Techniques and Applications.* New York: John Wiley and Sons, Inc. 1985.

Silverman, Barry G., ed. *Expert Systems for Business.* Reading, MA: Addison-Wesley Publishing Co., Inc., 1987.

Simon, Herbert A. *The Sciences of the Artificial* 2d ed. Cambridge, MA: MIT Press, 1981.

Tyugu, Enn. *Knowledge-Based Programming.* Reading, MA: Addison-Wesley Publishing Co., Inc., 1988.

Waterman, Donald. *A Guide to Expert Systems.* Reading, MA: Addison-Wesley Publishing Co., Inc., 1986.

Winston, Patrick Henry. *Artificial Intelligence,* 2d ed. Reading, MA: Addison-Wesley Publishing Co., Inc., 1981.

Intermediate Texts

Bond, Alan H., ed. and Gasser, Les. *Readings in Distributed Artificial Intelligence.* San Mateo, CA: Morgan Kaufmann Publishers, 1988.

Debenham, J. K. *Knowledge Systems Design.* Englewood Cliffs, NJ: Prentice Hall, Inc., 1989.

Delahaye, Jean-Paul. *Formal Methods in Artificial Intelligence.* New York: John Wiley and Sons, Inc., 1987.

Genesereth, Michael R., and Nilsson, Nils. *Logical Foundations of Artificial Intelligence.* San Mateo, CA: Morgan Kaufmann Publishers, Inc. 1987.

Hayes-Roth, Frederick; Waterman, Donald; and Lenat, Douglas. *Building Expert Systems.* Reading, MA: Addison-Wesley Publishing Co., Inc., 1983.

Holtzman, Samuel. *Intelligent Decision Systems.* Reading, MA: Addison-Wesley Publishing Co., Inc., 1989.

Huhns, Michael M. *Distributed Artificial Intelligence*. San Mateo, CA: Morgan Kaufmann, 1987.

Klahr, Philip, and Waterman, Donald, eds. *Expert Systems: Techniques, Tools and Applications ed*. Reading, MA: Addison-Wesley Publishing Co., Inc., 1986.

Manna, Zohar, and Waldinger, Richard. *The Logical Basis for Computer Programming*, vol. 2, *Deductive Systems*. Reading, MA: Addison-Wesley Publishing Co., Inc., 1990.

Michie, Donald. *Machine Intelligence*. London: Oxford University Press, 1988.

Nilsson, Nils J. *Problem-Solving Methods in Artificial Intelligence*. New York: McGraw-Hill, Inc., 1971.

Pearl, Judea. *Heuristics: Intelligent Search Strategies for Computer Problem Solving*. Reading, MA: Addison-Wesley Publishing Co., Inc., 1984.

Porter, Michael I. *Foundations of Cognitive Science*. Cambridge, MA: MIT Press, 1989.

Prerau, David S. *Developing and Managing Expert Systems: Proven Techniques for Business and Industry*. Reading, MA: Addison-Wesley Publishing Co., Inc., 1990.

Rich, Charles, and Waters, Richard C., eds. *Readings in Artificial Intelligence and Software Engineering*. San Mateo, CA: Morgan Kaufmann Publishers, Inc., 1986.

Rosenberg, Jerry M. *Dictionary of Artificial Intelligence and Robotics*. New York: John Wiley and Sons, Inc., 1986.

Schank, Roger C. *Dynamic Memory*. New York: Cambridge University Press, 1982.

Sharkey, N. E. ed. *Advances in Cognitive Science*. New York: John Wiley and Sons, Inc., 1986.

Shoham, Yoav. *Reasoning About Change*. Cambridge, MA: MIT Press, 1988.

Shrobe, Howard E., and The American Association for Artificial Intelligence, eds.. *Exploring Artificial Intelligence: Survey Talks from the National Conferences on Artificial Intelligence*. San Mateo, CA: Morgan Kaufmann, 1988.

Swift, K.G.. *Knowledge-Based Design for Manufacture*. Englewood Cliffs, NJ: Prentice Hall, Inc., 1987.

Thierauf, Robert J. *User-Orientation Decision Support Systems*. Englewood Cliffs, NJ: Prentice Hall, Inc., 1988.

Tricholy, Eric, and Orr, Joel N. *Computer-Integrated Manufacturing Handbook*. New York: McGraw-Hill, Inc., 1987.

Webber, Bonnie Lynn, and Nilsson, Nils J. *Readings in Artificial Intelligence*. San Mateo, CA: Morgan Kaufmann Publishers, Inc. 1981.

Winograd, Terry and Flores, Fernando. *Understanding Computers and Cognition*. Reading, MA: Addison-Wesley Publishing Co., Inc., 1986.

Winstanley, Graham. *Program Design for Knowledge Based Systems*. Wilmslow, UK: Sigma Press, 1987.

Bibel, W. and Jorrand, P., eds., *Fundamentals of Artificial Intelligence: An Advanced Course.* Berlin: Springer-Verlag, 1987.

Feigenbaum, Edward A., and Cohen, Paul R., eds. *The Handbook of Artificial Intelligence*, vol. 3. Los Altos, CA: William Kaufmann, Inc., 1982.

Ginsberg, Alan. *Automatic Refinement of Expert System Knowledge.* San Mateo, CA: Morgan Kaufmann, 1988.

Ginsberg, Matthew L. *Readings in Nonmonotonic Reasoning.* San Mateo, CA: Morgan Kaufmann, 1987.

Glorioso, Robert M., and Osorio, Fernando C. Colon. *Engineering Intelligent Systems.* Bedford, MA: Digital Press, 1980.

Kanal, Laveen, and Kumar, Vipin. *Search in Artificial Intelligence.* Berlin: Springer-Verlag, 1988.

Kowalik, J. S. *Coupling Symbolic and Numerical Computing in Expert Systems.* New York: Elsevier Science Publishers, 1988.

Kowalik, Janusz S. *Knowledge Based Problem Solving.* Englewood Cliffs, NJ: Prentice Hall, Inc., 1986.

Kowalski, Robert. *Logic for Problem Solving.* Amsterdam: Elsevier North-Holland, Inc., 1979.

Lemmer, John F., and Kanel, Laveen N., eds., *Uncertainty in Artificial Intelligence 2.* New York: Elsevier, 1988.

Lenat, Douglas B., and Guha, R. V. *Building Large Knowledge-Based Systems: Representation & Inference in the CYC Project.* Reading, MA: Addison-Wesley Publishing Co., Inc., 1990.

McClelland, James L.; Rumelhart, David E.; and The PDP Research Group. *Parallel Distributed Processing: Explorations in the Microstructure of Cognition,* vol. 1, *Foundations.* Cambridge, MA: MIT Press, 1986.

Minker, Jack, ed. *Foundations of Deductive Databases and Logic Programming.* San Mateo, CA: Morgan Kaufmann Publishers, 1987.

Pearl, Judea. *Probabilistic Reasoning in Intelligent Systems: Networks of Plausible Inference.* San Mateo, CA: Morgan Kaufmann, 1988.

Politakis, Peter. *Empirical Analysis for Expert Systems.* Boston: Pitman, 1985.

Press, S. James. *Bayesian Statistics: Principles, Models and Applications.* New York: John Wiley and Sons, Inc., 1989.

Sager, Naomi. *Natural Language Information Processing.* Reading, MA: Addison-Wesley Publishing Co., Inc., 1981.

Widman, Lawrence E.; Loparo, Kenneth A.; and Nielsen, Norman R., eds. *Artificial Intelligence, Simulation & Modeling.* New York: John Wiley and Sons, Inc., 1989.

Wilensky, Robert. *Planning and Understanding.* Reading, MA: Addison-Wesley Publishing Co., Inc., 1983.

Winograd, Terry. *Language as a Cognitive Process.* vol. 1, *Syntax.* Reading, MA: Addison-Wesley Publishing Co., Inc., 1983.

Yonezawa, Akinori, and Tokoro, Mario. *Object-Oriented Concurrent Programming.* Cambridge, MA: MIT Press, 1987.

Bachant, J., and McDermott, J. "R1 Revisited Four Years in the Trenches." *AI Magazine*, vol. 5, no. 3 (1984).

Bachant, J., and Soloway, E. "The Engineering of XCON." *Communications of the ACM*, vol. 32, no. 3, (1989).

Barker, Virginia E., and O'Connor, Dennis. "Expert Systems for Configuration at Digital: XCON and Beyond." *Communications of the ACM*, vol. 32, no. 3 (1989).

Clancey, William J. *Knowledge-Based Tutoring: The Guidon Program.* Cambridge, MA: MIT Press, 1987.

Cohn, A. G. and Thomas, J. R. *Artificial Intelligence and Its Applications.* New York: John Wiley and Sons, Inc., 1986.

Ernst, Christian J. *Management Expert Systems.* Reading, MA: Addison-Wesley Publishing Co., Inc., 1988.

Gale, William A., ed. *Artificial Intelligence & Statistics.* Reading, MA: Addison-Wesley Publishing Co., Inc., 1986.

Gardner, Anne von der Lieth. *An Artificial Intelligence Approach to Legal Reasoning.* Cambridge, MA: MIT Press, 1987.

Hertz, David Bendel. *The Expert Executive: Using AI and Expert Systems for Financial Management, Marketing, Production, and Strategy.* New York: John Wiley and Sons, Inc., 1988.

Kaewert, J., and Frost, J. *Developing Expert Systems for Manufacturing, A Case Study Approach.* New York: McGraw-Hill, Inc. 1990.

Kearlsey, Greg, ed. *Artificial Intelligence and Instruction.* Reading, MA: Addison-Wesley Publishing Co., Inc., 1987.

Keraunoir, E. J. and Johnson, L. *Competent Expert Systems: A Case Study in Fault Diagnosis.* New York: McGraw-Hill, Inc., 1986.

Krakauer, Jake, ed. *Smart Manufacturing with Artificial Intelligence.* Society of Manufacturing Engineers, 1987.

Krig, Jiri, ed., *Knowledge-Based Expert Systems in Industry.* Chichester, UK: Ellis Horwood Limited, 1987.

Kusiak, Andrew, ed. *Artificial Intelligence: Implications for CIM.* Berlin: Springer-Verlag, 1988.

Kusiak, Andrew. *Intelligent Manufacturing Systems.* Englewood Cliffs, NJ: Prentice Hall, Inc., 1990.

Lawler, Robert W., ed. *Artificial Intelligence and Education.* Norwood, NJ: Ablex Publishing, 1987.

Liebowitz, Jay, ed., *Expert Systems Applications to Telecommunications.* New York: John Wiley and Sons, Inc., 1988.

McDermott, J. "R1's Formative Years." *AI Magazine*, vol. 2, no. 2 (1981).

Mumford, Enid, and MacDonald, W. Bruce. *XSEL's Progress: The Continuing Journey of an Expert System.* New York: John Wiley and Sons, Inc., 1989.

Niwa, Kiyoshi. *Knowledge-Based Risk Management in Engineering.* New York: John Wiley and Sons, Inc., 1989.

Pau, L. F. ed. *Artificial Intelligence in Economics and Management.* New York: Elsevier, 1987.

Quinlan, J. Ross, ed. *Applications of Expert Systems Based on the Proceedings of the Second Australian Conference.* Reading, MA: Addison-Wesley Publishing Co., Inc., 1987.

Rauch-Hindin, Wendy B. *A Guide to Commercial Artificial Intelligence.* Englewood Cliffs, NJ: Prentice Hall, Inc., 1988.

Reggia, James A., and Tuhrim, Stanley. *Computer-Assisted Medical Decision Making.* Berlin: Springer-Verlag, 1985.

Reitman, Walter, ed. *Artificial Intelligence Applications for Business.* Norwood, NJ: Ablex Publishing, 1984.

Schoen, Seymour, and Sykes, Wendell G. *Putting Artificial Intelligence to Work: Evaluating and Implementing Business Applications.* New York: John Wiley and Sons, Inc., 1987.

Sleeman, D., and Brown, J. S., eds. *Intelligent Tutoring Systems.* New York: Academic Press, Inc., 1982.

Slocum, Jonathan, ed. *Machine Translation Systems.* New York: Cambridge University Press, 1988.

Turban, Efraim. *Decision Support and Expert Systems: Management Support Systems.* Riverside, NJ: Macmillan, Inc., 1990.

Wenger, Etienne. *Artificial Intelligence and Tutoring Systems: Computational and Cognitive Approaches to the Communication of Knowledge.* San Mateo, CA: Morgan Kaufmann, 1987.

Wolfgram, Deborah D.; Dear, Teresa J.; and Galbraith, Craig S. *Expert Systems for The Technical Professional.* New York: John Wiley and Sons, Inc., 1987.

Wright, Paul K., and Bourne, David A. *Manufacturing Intelligence.* Reading, MA: Addison-Wesley Publishing Co., Inc., 1988.

Languages and Tools

Bundy, Alan, ed. *Catalogue of Artificial Intelligence Tools,* 2d ed. Berlin: Springer-Verlag, 1986.

Clocksin, W. F., and Mellish, C. S. *Programming in PROLOG,* 3d ed. Berlin: Springer-Verlag, 1987.

Cooper, Thomas A., and Wogrin, Nancy. *Rule-Based Programming with OPS5.* San Mateo, CA: Morgan Kaufmann, 1989.

Harmon, Paul, et al. *Expert Systems, Tools and Applications.* New York: John Wiley and Sons, Inc., 1988.

O'Shea, Tim, and Eisenstadt, Marc. *Artificial Intelligence: Tools, Techniques and Applications.* New York: Harper & Row, 1984.

Sriram, D., and Adey, R. A., eds. *Artificial Intelligence in Engineering: Tools and Techniques.* Boston: Computational Mechanics Publications, 1987.

Steele, Guy L., Jr. *Common LISP: The Language.* Bedford, MA: Digital Press, 1990.

Tello, Ernest R. *Object-Oriented Programming for Artificial Intelligence: A Guide to Tools and System Design.* Reading, MA: Addison-Wesley Publishing Co., Inc., 1989.

Knowledge Representation

Amble, Tore. *Logic Programming and Knowledge Engineering.* Reading, MA: Addison-Wesley Publishing Co., Inc., 1987.

Bobrow, Daniel G., and Collins, Allan. *Representation and Understanding.* New York: Academic Press, Inc., 1975.

Ellis, Charlie. *Expert Knowledge and Explanation: The Knowledge-Language Interface.* Chichester, UK: Ellis Horwood Limited, 1989.

Graham, Ian, and Jones, Peter L. *Expert Systems: Knowledge, Uncertainity and Decision.* New York: Chapman and Hall, 1988.

Ringland, G. A., and Duce, D. A. *Approaches to Knowledge Representation: An Introduction.* New York: John Wiley and Sons, Inc., 1988.

Sowa, John. *Conceptual Structures.* Reading, MA: Addison-Wesley Publishing Co., Inc., 1984.

Knowledge Acquisition

Berwick, Robert. *The Acquisiton of Syntactic Knowledge.* Cambridge, MA: MIT Press, 1985.

Boose, John. *Expertise Transfer for Expert System Design.* New York: Elsevier Science Publishing Company, 1986.

Hart, Anna. *Knowledge Acquisition for Expert Systems.* New York: McGraw-Hill, Inc., 1987.

Kidd, Alison L. *Knowledge Acquisition for Expert Systems.* New York: Plenum Press, 1987.

Marcus, Sandra, ed. *Automating Knowledge for Expert Systems.* Boston: Kluwer Academic, 1988.

McGraw, Karen L. *Knowledge Acquisition: Principles and Guidelines.* Englewood Cliffs, NJ: Prentice Hall, Inc., 1989.

User Interface

Hartson, H. Rex, ed. *Advances in Human-Computer Interaction,* vol. 1. Norwood, NJ: Ablex Publishing Corp., 1985.

Hawley, Robert, ed. *Artificial Intelligence Programming Environments* Chichester, UK: Ellis Horwood Limited, 1987.

Hendler, James A., ed. *Expert Systems: The User Interface.* Norwood, NJ: Ablex Publishing Corporation, 1988.

Ledgard, Henry, et al. *Directions in Human Factors for Interactive Systems.* Berlin: Springer-Verlag, 1981.

Shneiderman, Ben. *Designing the User Interface: Strategies for Effective Human-Computer Interaction.* Reading, MA: Addison-Wesley Publishing Co., Inc., 1987.

Integration

Brodie, Michael, and Mylopoulos, John. *On Knowledge Base Management Systems: Integrating Artificial Intelligence and Database Technologies.* Berlin: Springer-Verlag, 1986.

Gallagher, John P. *Knowledge Systems for Business: Integrating Expert Systems and MIS.* Englewood Cliffs, NJ: Prentice Hall, Inc., 1988.

Gardarin, Georges, and Valduriez, Patrick. *Relational Databases and Knowledge Bases.* Reading, MA: Addison-Wesley Publishing Co., Inc., 1989.

Mylopolus, John, ed. *Readings in Artificial Intelligence and Databases.* San Mateo, CA: Morgan-Kaufmann, 1989.

Parsaye, Kamran; Chignelland, Mark; and Khoshafian, Setrag. *Intelligent Databases: Object-Oriented, Deductive Hypermedia Technologies.* New York: John Wiley and Sons, Inc., 1989.

Uhr, Leonard. *Multi-Computer Architectures for Artificial Intelligence.* New York: John Wiley and Sons, Inc., 1987.

Ullman, Jeffrey D. *Principles of Database and Knowledge-Base Systems.* Rockville, MD: Computer Science Press, 1988.

Managing Expert Systems

Bryant, Nigel. *Managing Expert Systems.* New York: John Wiley and Sons, Inc., 1988.

DeSalvo, Daniel A., and Liebowitz, Jay. *Managing Artificial Intelligence and Expert Systems.* Englewood Cliffs, NJ: Yourdon Press, 1990.

Induction and Learning

Bolc, Leonard ed. *Computational Models of Learning.* Berlin: Springer-Verlag, 1987.

Holland, John H.; Holyoak, Keith F.; Nisbett, Richard; and Thagard, Paul R. *Induction: Processes of Inference, Learning and Discovery.* Cambridge, MA: MIT Press, 1986.

Michalski, Ryszard S.; Carbonell, Jaime G.; and Mitchell, Tom M., eds. *Machine Learning.* Palo Alto, CA: Tioga Press, 1983.

Riesbeck, Christopher K., and Schank, Roger C. *Inside Case-Based Reasoning.* Hillsdale, NJ: Lawrence Erlbaum Associates, 1989.

Implications of Expert Systems

Beerel, Annabel C. *Expert Systems: Strategic Implications and Applications.* New York: Halsted Press, 1987.

Davies, R., ed. *Intelligent Information Systems: Progress and Prospects.* Chichester, UK: Ellis Horwood Limited, 1986.

Feigenbaum, Edward A., and McCorduck, Pamela. *The Fifth Generation.* Reading, MA: Addison-Wesley Publishing Co., Inc., 1983.

Feigenbaum, Edward A., et al. *The Rise of the Expert Company*. New York: Random House, Inc., 1988.

Gevarter, William B. *Intelligent Machines*. Englewood Cliffs, NJ: Prentice Hall, Inc., 1985.

Greene, Richard. *Implementing Japanese AI Techniques: Turning the Tables for a Winning Strategy*. New York: McGraw-Hill, Inc., 1990.

McCorduck, Pamela. *Machines Who Think*. San Francisco, CA: W. H. Freeman and Company, 1979.

Minsky, Marvin. *The Society of Mind*. New York: Simon and Schuster, Inc., 1986.

Partridge, D. *Artificial Intelligence Applications in the Future of Software Engineering*. Chichester, UK: Ellis Horwood, 1986.

Weizenbaum, Joseph. *Computer Power and Human Reason: From Judgment To Calculation*. San Francisco, CA: W. H. Freeman and Company, 1976.

Winston, Patrick H., and Prendergast, Karen A., eds. *The AI Business*. Cambridge, MA: MIT Press, 1984.

Yazdani, M., and Narayanan, A., eds. *Artificial Intelligence: Human Effects*. New York: John Wiley and Sons, Inc., 1984.

Zuboff, Shoshano. *In the Age of the Smart Machine*. New York: Basic Books, Inc., 1988.

Index

subjective criteria, 147
   unbounded domain, 146–147
   underestimating integration and
      hybridization, 142–146
Procedural knowledge, 15
Procedural review, 114–115, 117
Process control expert systems, 9
Production systems, 18
Programming
   linear, 4–5
   scientific, 3–4
   time spent on, 14
Project
   beginning, 49–57
   flow of, 11
   management of, 15
Project participants, 11
   knowledge engineer's relationship
      with, 49–52, 80–81, 138–141,
      154–156
   plan for first meeting of, 54–57
   See also Interviews
Prolog, 24, 106
Propagation of probability, 22
Prospecting, 31–48
   analysis stage of, 31, 34–40
   configuration stage of, 31, 40–42
   defined, 11, 31
   diagnosis stage of, 31–34
   sample reports, 43–48
   time spent on, 14
Prototyping, 11, 53, 187–189
   plan for, 54–56
   standalone system in, 51, 54
Proxy systems, 9, 67–68
Purposes, 8, 9, 66–69

Questions, 34–40, 77–78
   exclusionary, 34–36
   financial, 36–38
   technical, 39–40

Reasoning, 18
Reports
   knowledge acquisition, 82–88
   prospecting, 43–48
Requisition, 16
Results, 16
Reviews
   ancillary, 116
   expansion, 116
   integration, 116
   personnel, 116
   position, 115–116, 117–118

   procedural, 114–115, 117
   task, 113–114
   technical, 115, 117
   temporal, 113, 114
Right-hand side (RHS), 16
Rules, 16–17, 18, 26–27
   in coding, 186–187
   in knowledge acquisition, 80–81
   in knowledge representation, 95–99

Savings, 110–112
Scanned images, 126
Schedule
   of domain experts, 40–41
   establishing, 53
   for interviews, 74
   of knowledge engineers, 14–15
Scheduling/planning systems, 64–65
Schemes, 89
Scientific programming (SP), vs. expert
    systems, 3–4
Scoping the problem, 74–75
Second generation, 20
Selective systems, 60–62
Semantic nets, 105–106
Sensors, 9
Situations, 16
Sixth generation, 21
Slang terms, 79
Slots, 100
Socratic tutors, 67
Software
   available, 34–35
   generations of, 20–21
   integration of, 143–146
Speculative systems, 68–69
Standalone expert system, 14, 51, 54,
   142
Status, loss of, 138–141
Strategic openings, 33
Structure of expert systems, 9
Sub-experts, 40
Subjective criteria, 147
Subobject, 102
Substitution, 17
Superstition, 27
Supposition, 16
Surface knowledge, 11

Tape recorder, 81, 179
Task reviews, 113–114
Technical review, 115, 117
Technical terms, 79
Technology transfer, 14

Printed in Dunstable, United Kingdom